Co-Designers

"This book is more than a conversation starter; it is a conversation changer. A designer and an ethnographer, Loukissas provides a rare dual vision on how simulation changes how we build and think about building. Elegant. Sophisticated. A must-read across a range of fields in science and technology studies and design."

Sherry Turkle, Abby Rockefeller Mauzé Professor of the Social Studies of Science and Technology, Massachusetts Institute of Technology, USA

Designers employ a variety of tools and techniques for speculating about buildings before they are built. In their simplest form, these are personal thought experiments. However, embracing advanced computer simulations means engaging a network of specialized people and powerful machines. In this book, Yanni Alexander Loukissas demonstrates that new tools have profound implications for the social distribution of design work; computer simulations are technologies for collective imagination.

Organized around the accounts of professional designers engaged in a high-stakes competition to redefine their work for the technological moment, this book explores the emerging cultures of computer simulation in architecture. Not only architects, but acousticians, fire safety engineers, and sustainability experts see themselves as co-designers in architecture, engaging new technologies for simulation in an evolving search for the roles and relationships that can bring them both professional acceptance and greater control over design. By illustrating how practices of simulation inform the social relationships and professional distinctions that define contemporary architecture, the book reveals cultural transformations taking place in design practice today.

Yanni Alexander Loukissas is a Postdoctoral Associate in the Program in Science, Technology, and Society (STS) at MIT. He has also been a Visiting Lecturer in the Department of Architecture at Cornell University. He holds an SM and a PhD in Design and Computation from the Massachusetts Institute of Technology (MIT), as well as a BArch from Cornell University.

Co-Designers

Cultures of Computer Simulation in Architecture

Yanni Alexander Loukissas

Routledge
Taylor & Francis Group
LONDON AND NEW YORK

First published 2012
by Routledge
4 Park Square, Milton Park, Abingdon, Oxon OX14 4RN
605 Third Avenue, New York, NY 10017

Routledge is an imprint of the Taylor & Francis Group, an informa business

British Library Cataloguing in Publication Data
A catalogue record for this book is available from the British Library

Library of Congress Cataloging in Publication Data
Loukissas, Yanni A. (Yanni Alexander)
Co-designers : cultures of computer simulation in architecture / Yanni Alexander Loukissas.
p. cm.
Includes bibliographical references and index.
1. Architecture and technology. 2. Computer simulation.
3. Architectural design. 4. Architectural practice. I. Title.
II. Title: Cultures of computer simulation in architecture.
NA2543.T43L68 2012
720'.285–dc23
2011040909

ISBN: 978-0-415-59227-7 (hbk)
ISBN: 978-0-415-59228-4 (pbk)
ISBN: 978-0-203-12306-5 (ebk)

Typeset in ITC Stone Serif
by RefineCatch Limited, Bungay, Suffolk

to my parents

Contents

List of Illustration Credits

Figure 1 Photograph by Henk Snoek, Courtesy of Arup.

Figure 2 Photograph, Courtesy of Arup.

Figure 3 Drawing by Robert Maillart, Courtesy of Maillart Archives.

Figure 4 Photograph, Courtesy of Arup.

Figure 5 Simulation, Courtesy of Arup.

Figure 6 Photograph © Erick Buck, Courtesy of Arup.

Figure 7 Illustrations by George Saunders from *A Treatise on Theatres*, London: I. and J. Taylor, 1790, Plate I.

Figure 8 Sketch, Courtesy of Arup.

Figure 9 Photograph, Courtesy of Arup.

Figure 10 Photograph, Courtesy of Arup.

Figure 11 Photograph, Courtesy of Arup.

Figure 12 Smoke simulation frames, Courtesy of Arup.

Figure 13 Structural simulation, Courtesy of Arup.

Figure 14 Realtime simulation, Courtesy of Arup.

Figure 15 Drawings, Courtesy of Arup.

Figure 16 Photograph by Don McPhedron, Australian Photographic Agency – 03870 Mitchell Library, State Library of New South Wales.

Figure 17 Photograph of spherical model, by Jørn Utzon Courtesy of Jan Utzon and the National Library of Australia.

Figure 18 Photograph, Courtesy of Arup.

Figure 19 Photograph, Courtesy of Arup.

Figure 20 Environmental simulations, Courtesy of Arup.

Figure 21 Photograph, Courtesy of Arup.

Figure 22 Photograph, Courtesy of Arup.

Figure 23 Light simulation variations, Courtesy of Arup.

Figure 24 Image, Courtesy of Milena Zindiovic.

Preface

For designers in architecture, taking up a new technology means establishing a creative dialog. Savvy practitioners understand this implicitly. They see themselves as *co-designers*, evaluating existing conditions and imagining alternatives in response to changing social and technological conditions. Meanwhile, many books about design explain technology as either pragmatic or ideological; in either case, a question of individual preference. Yet engaging a technology means negotiating a system of social relationships. In this book, I explore a shift in the work of designers, from manual traditions to virtual tools, and accompanying concerns about the redistribution of control and responsibility. I am writing for two audiences: non-practitioners who want to understand how computer simulations are shaping new relationships in design and practitioners who know how, but wonder "So what?"

In 2004, early on during my doctoral studies at the Massachusetts Institute of Technology (MIT), I joined an interdisciplinary research project to examine the role of technologies for visualization and simulation in professional changes within four domains: architecture, nuclear weapons design, life science, and aviation. This project, entitled "Information Technologies and Professional Identity: A Comparative Study of Virtuality" was initiated in the MIT Program in Science, Technology, and Society and funded by the National Science Foundation (Grant No. 0220347). The project was led by five faculty members: Sherry Turkle, Susan Silbey, David Mindell, Hugh Gusterson, and Joseph Dumit. Natasha Myers was my pre-doctoral co-fellow on the project. Across all four fields, our study revealed how simulations are transforming professional experience – the means by which professionals develop intuition and expertise. My dissertation, and now this book, follow from that study and deepen it in the area of architecture. Any opinions, findings, and conclusions or recommendations expressed in this material are those of the author and do not necessarily reflect the views of the National Science Foundation. Some of the material on architects has already been published in an essay entitled "Keepers of the Geometry," in *Simulation and its Discontents*, edited by Sherry Turkle and published by The MIT Press in 2009.[1]

In this book, I use the accounts of practitioners in a range of design offices, primarily in the United States and England, to explore how technologies for simulation have opened up new identities for designers. I examine these accounts, not somehow to uncover in an absolute sense how architecture has changed, but to understand the role of technology in professional claims, both legitimate and spurious, about what constitutes design, what it does, and who can do it. Attaining empirical evidence of competing conceptions of design is not simple. It is not sufficient merely to observe practitioners at work. Observation alone cannot penetrate into the meaning of professional practices. Nor is it possible to get at these conceptions through standardized questions. Questionnaires run the risk of being too narrow in their terms and framing to capture the richness of professional changes. My approach draws upon traditions of ethnography, the interpretive methodology of anthropologists. I use ethnography to identify watershed episodes in practice that frame recent changes in the way that professionals see their work.

My evidence comes from the oral and material cultures of design, including interviews, observations, simulations, journal articles, technical papers, books, images, and commentaries on practice in popular media. Among the most important resources in my writing are my field notes from more than 100 in-depth, unstructured interviews with practitioners.[2] In these interviews, I try to uncover ways of thinking about design that I was not necessarily aware of or prepared to interrogate. This method requires careful probing, reflection, and redirection during the course of each interview. In these sessions, which last from one to three hours, my goal is to learn about personal conceptions supported by new technological practices. I develop lengthy field notes from these interviews, which are then subject to analysis in the context of additional evidence from observation, project documentation, and first-hand experience with simulations. Finally, instead of summarizing the results of my interviews, which would dilute the subtle discourse of practitioners, I select salient excerpts that illustrate the competing notions of design I seek to characterize. Because of the unrepeatable nature of this method, its results are subject to serious criticism, against which the only defense is a sensitive interpretation of the evidence and a rigorous account of the context of my work.

I use a combination of real names and pseudonyms in this book. This is unavoidable, due to the combination of heterogeneous contexts that I wish to present. It is nearly impossible to present well-known architecture projects without revealing real names, particularly the names of associated institutions and their principals or directors. However, I use pseudonyms whenever possible, to give a degree of protection to subjects who have not already become part of the historical record, and to put the focus on social dynamics, rather than real people. I also treat contemporary informants and historical subjects differently. All of my informants, the individuals whom I interviewed and observed directly, have pseudonyms, although in some cases I still use the real names of their firms. However, I do not anonymize historical subjects, as in the case of Ove Arup, founder of Arup, because my sources for such references are almost always already public.

This book was made possible by the help of many institutions, informants, advisors, collaborators, friends, and family members. A full list of these contributors is impossible to compile. However, I wish to thank a few special individuals, those who had a profound influence on the final product. I must first thank my informants, those who provided the grist for my mill. I have kept their names confidential, but I would like to express my gratitude to them. In my study of Arup, I owe special thanks to a few individuals: Jessica Strauss, a classmate from Cornell University, introduced me to key members of the firm and helped me to earn their trust. Daniel Imade helped me gather and attain permissions for many of the images in the book. Mahadev Raman, the director of the American offices of Arup, championed my study before the Arup Board of Trustees. Sincere thanks to all the other designers and design offices that contributed to my research but are not mentioned by name in order to preserve their anonymity.

Among those who helped me from MIT, I wish to thank David Mindell, my post-doctoral supervisor, for offering the encouragement, the proper intellectual climate, and not insignificantly, the time to convert my dissertation into a book. I completed this book while I was a member of Mindell's budding Laboratory for Automation, Robotics, and Society (LARS), between test flights and our meetings with Apollo astronauts. Additional thanks to the members of LARS, particularly Zara Mirmalek, for their continual support. My dissertation committee members have also remained active during this latest phase of research and writing. William Porter has continued to be a close advisor, interlocutor, and confidant. I could not have asked for a more patient and sagacious guide through the difficulties of becoming a researcher. I owe much of my thinking on technology and self to Sherry Turkle. She also inspired my interest in ethnography, taught me how to do it, and gave me the confidence to see this work through. William Mitchell passed away while this book was still in its early phases; however, during the time I had with him, Mitchell made many profound and pragmatic contributions to this work. Edith Ackermann has been a source of inspiration and insight since my first days at MIT. She helped me to see design through "her lenses," the lenses of the social scientist, and convinced me that I could make a contribution to social science, using the lenses of the designer.

Furthermore, I wish to acknowledge the faculty, staff, and students of MIT, particularly those in the Department of Architecture, the Media Lab, and the Program in Science, Technology, and Society. They provided the ideal working environment for any ethnographer/designer/technologist. Thanks also to the Cornell University Department of Architecture, which supported me as a visiting lecturer for two years while I first imagined how my dissertation might become a book, and to the University of Cambridge, which hosted me while I conducted fieldwork in England. William Fawcett, my informal advisor at Cambridge, and his wife, Di Haigh, were more than intellectual and cultural guides to those environs; they made me feel like a part of the family. At Routledge, I would like to thank Kyle Duggan, Fran Ford, and Laura Williamson in particular for their feedback and enduring patience.

I must thank the individuals who were generous enough to read this book in its awkward early drafts: Daniel Cardoso, Nick Gayeski, Terry Knight, David Mindell, William Porter, David Salomon, and Sherry Turkle. I hope you will recognize in the text my ongoing dialog with your comments. My most careful reader has been Marilyn Levine, a coach and eventual collaborator whom I met through the MIT Writing Center. She has skillfully steered me through the final stages of completing this book and pushed me to improve the clarity of the writing and the consistency of the voice in each sentence. Any lumps that are left are due to my stubbornness alone.

Finally, my family and friends have provided crucial emotional support throughout my research and writing. My sister, Jennifer Loukissas, her husband, Doug Lynott, and their son, Michael, have cheered me on with particular enthusiasm. However, I owe the greatest debts to my mother, Lynne Randy Loukissas, and my father, Philippos Loukissas. Sadly, my father, who nudged me to become a designer in the first place, has declined into Alzheimer's disease during the years it has taken me to write these words. If I have one regret, it is that I did not finish this book quickly enough for him to read it.

Chapter 1

Introducing the Electronic Brain

On November 17, 1963, members of the international design consultancy, Arup, convened at their central offices in London for a "Symposium on the Use of Computers."[3] A decade earlier, the computer did not exist as a commercial product, but participants at the symposium were already talking about it as a necessary part of their work as technical advisors in architecture.[4] By then, some members of Arup were working closely with the Danish architect Jørn Utzon on the use of computing to conduct structural calculations for the notoriously complex Sydney Opera House roofs. In that project and many that followed, the computer was burdened by enormous expectations. At the introduction to the symposium, it was heralded as "the electronic brain of popular imagination," and its presence was treated with a mixture of excitement and anxiety.[5] However, these were early days in the history of computing in architecture. The participants, mostly engineers, were only beginning to test out ideas about how the computer might change the field and their professional roles within it.

The symposium attendees contemplated the possibility that the computer might enable a new range of building designs: "The engineer would be free to give more of his time to more interesting and complicated projects."[6] They speculated that it could affect the way engineers think: "The very fact that one would be using a computer ought to make one think systematically about what one was doing."[7] They also agreed that the computer would necessitate new roles in the office – programming in particular, which was described as a "completely new job."[8] One engineer exclaimed, "If we did start using computers, special men would develop in our office," at which everyone in attendance laughed, but they understood exactly what he meant.[9] "We needed people with this specialized knowledge to act as a link between us and our problems and the computer."[10] Though still enigmatic, the new machine suggested all these possibilities at once: a new range of forms, new ways of knowing, and new kinds of professionals in architecture.[11]

Across disciplines, computing is redefining the relationships and conceptual distinctions that define professional work.[12] In this book, I examine

Figure 1
A hybrid structural simulation of the Sydney Opera House roofs undergoing stress distribution testing by Arup, in collaboration with the Southampton University structural laboratory.

cultural transformations in architecture that are developing along with computer simulations. Engineers, architects, and others in the field are making trade-offs between manual traditions of design and new technologies for simulation. Historically, practitioners have developed a variety of tools and techniques for sharing imaginations, and even experiences, of buildings before they are built. In their simplest form, designers' simulations can be personal thought experiments or mental images. But creating advanced computer simulations means engaging a network of people and powerful machines. Indeed, new technologies have profound implications for the social distribution of work: computer simulations are technologies for collective imagination.[13]

Simulations performed on computers are used to forecast a range of behaviors in buildings: structural, visual, and acoustical, among others. They transform quantitative models of building physics into qualitative, sensory experiences. Internally, simulations contain only abstract, symbolic representations. However, they create convincing sensorial events for audiences varying from art critics to government regulators. Computer simulations have given rise to new organizations of technical and creative practitioners in

Figure 2
Ove Arup on top of Coventry Cathedral.

architecture, making the field an important site for studying the professional implications of advanced technologies. Architecture can tell us much about the changing role of human presence in the face of increasing simulation in the workplace.

Assertions at the Arup symposium about the pitfalls and opportunities presented by early computers were recorded in a company newsletter.[14] In particular, the newsletter makes note of the deeply held reservations and fears of practitioners: "There were agitated movements that indicated that the discussion was on the boil."[15] Ove Arup, founder of the firm bearing his name, was among the most resistant of the participants. "Design by computer was impossible," he argued.[16] "A computer has to be told what to do." Arup's remarks suggest that the computer and the designer are at odds. "Design is visual. You can see immediately whether something is sensible or not." To overlook this distinction was to put the designer in jeopardy of being mechanized. Arup dramatized the implications of mechanization by making an analogy between the computerized design office and the workings of an automated farm owned by a friend of his. "Those unfortunate cows that do not conform, those that have too much or too little milk for the machine, have to be got rid of!" Ove Arup's troubled comments highlight the degree to which the symposium was about the implications of computing for human workers.[17] Many of the symposium's attendees were fearful that the computer could come to "dominate" their lives.[18] One defiantly asked, "[W]hy should a computer determine the design?"[19]

This historical scene captures not only apprehension, but the early hopes of practitioners in architecture – that computers would allow humans to focus on the important aspects of design and delegate the rest to machines. "It may eventually take the odious routines off our hands," suggested one symposium participant.[20] The idea that computing might take some aspects of design out of the hands of humans has since been a source of enthusiasm, but also of deep concern. Engineers and architects have struggled to define the enduring importance of human presence, judgment, and skill in design. Even today, in preparing the next generation of practitioners, they carefully consider which human capabilities might be most complementary to the computer: should students of design be trained in construction, the arts, or computer programming? Accounts from the symposium only foreshadow a wave of narratives that practitioners have since developed to think about architecture and themselves in relationship to the machine. By examining these narratives closely, we can see emerging patterns in professional life and reflect on changing notions of identity, knowledge, and form.

Boundaries of Architecture

Beyond their explicit assertions about the capacities and limits of computers, voices from the symposium carried implicit questions about the boundaries of architecture as a discipline and its stability over time. How might architecture change in relationship to computing? What, if anything, should endure? In this book, I consider what the accounts of a new class of architects and engineers can tell us about how the meaning of architecture is negotiated in the technological moment: as a set of professional identities, a system of knowledge, and a formal approach to the material world. This is a cultural study of technology. Changing human–machine–environment relationships in architecture are an indication of broader shifts in the locus of decision-making.

Since the time of the symposium, new roles have developed around the use of computers in architecture. And yet, the professional boundaries that separate architects from engineers have never been stable. Historian Andrew Saint writes of architects and engineers as siblings, "perpetually learning how to live together."[21] Today, in 2012, both disciplines use computer simulations to negotiate this relationship. Whether by mandate, or through their enthusiasm for the new medium, a number of architects are using these technologies to enrich their technical understanding of buildings, since the

Enlightenment the traditional domain of engineers. Reciprocally, some engineers are using computer simulations to meet architects on their own aesthetic terms.

In the context of this continual flux, a more inclusive category is needed to account for all those who bring their aesthetic, technical, scientific, or political skills to bear in building design. I assert that these practitioners are all designers, or co-designers, in their way: they are creative, but partial, contributors to the work of imagining architecture. I use the term designer liberally, not to whitewash the differences between practitioners, but rather to emphasize the creative contributions of each and to forestall ready-made attributions of authorship in new configurations of humans and machines.

Understanding the implications of computer simulations requires a broad view of how they affect systems of relationships. It is not enough simply to talk about these technologies in terms of one person at a machine. In addition to many varieties of architects and engineers, those participants who are seemingly on the fringe of design – including regulators, contractors, technology developers, and researchers – are all designers in their own right. These participants have found diverse ways of staying in the loop and maintaining influential roles in the field. However, this book does not seek to tell the stories of all designers. That is a much more ambitious project. Instead, it focuses on an emerging faction of practitioners, those who define themselves and their work explicitly in relationship to computer simulations. Their stories offer crucial insights into the rapidly changing social and technological system of architecture practice.

Theorist Herbert Simon may have defined design in its broadest sense in *The Sciences of the Artificial,* as any activity where an existing state is transformed to a preferred state.[22] In practice, the activities labeled design and the people who call themselves designers are not nearly as broadly constituted. Therefore, for the sake of this book, I have had to establish some limits on what I consider to be design. However, future studies would do well to question the boundaries that I draw here.

In architecture, which deals with the large-scale transformation of human environments, I take design to be the manipulation of representations of environments: plans, sections, models, diagrams, and other "intermediary objects."[23] Computer simulations are also intermediary. They are part of the evolving toolkit that practitioners use to establish virtual sites in which designs can be tested before they are built. They exist between conception and construction, but also between professional groups. However, computer simulations can be different things to different groups: tools for exploration, verification, reflection, or simply communication. In this sense, a definition of simulation is not easily held down. In fact, as Wittgenstein observes, words only gravitate toward stable meanings in dialog, and even then, personal interpretations come into play. The search for simulation's meaning in practice is a kind of "language game."[24] The term simulation, as applied in everyday design settings, is only as well defined as it needs to be to enable an exchange.

While later in the book, I will explain the kinds of exchange that simulations enable, I employ the term now in reference to a type of representation that maps closely onto how people perceive their environments. The simulations addressed in this book are not the abstract models that architects make for themselves as form-finding devices, nor the exclusively numerical spreadsheets that engineers create routinely. Those are important representations indeed, but they are not my focus.[25] Instead, I concentrate on the computer simulations that motivate broad consensus through virtual experiences of alternate possible realities.

There is also a history to the separation of design (the transformation of representations) from construction (the transformation of materials), which has technical, economic, and deeply professional motivations that echo some of the themes highlighted in this book.[26] However, rather than consider people who make buildings, I focus on people who make building representations. But even when these distinctions are taken for granted, divisions proliferate. Professionals jockey for jurisdiction over the means of representation. Creative and technical tasks are differentiated in inconsistent ways. From project to project, architects and engineers must look for ways in which they can represent architecture in order to gain a professional upper hand. Conceptions of architecture, its parts, practices, and purposes, are under continual negotiation through representations. Computer simulations become players within these negotiations. As such, I am attentive to the ways in which professionals use simulations strategically. Tracking contemporary professional narratives reveals how computer simulations are used to reframe architecture for purposes of professional positioning.[27] Such technologies are configurations of both materials and human relationships.[28] We need to assess which claims about computing suggest new configurations for designers, and which ones serve to maintain old hierarchies and disciplinary boundaries.

By the time of the 1963 symposium, Ove Arup and his colleagues had already started to define themselves in relation to the perceived capabilities of early computers. Yet they were only beginning to test out ideas about how to appropriate computing to reframe architecture. Today, computers are being adopted by designers to make new claims about buildings. Architects are adopting visualization to image architecture with unprecedented realism. Acousticians are using auralization to help their clients listen to buildings before they are built. Structural engineers are using finite element analysis to discover a new range of optimal shapes.

Many designers have reflected on the diffusion of computing into architecture.[29] However, they have done so in terms which are predominantly instrumental. When theorists of architecture write about the implications of the digital, they often miss the changes that redefine the profession at a cultural level: how good form is assessed, how identity is professed, and how knowledge is produced.[30] The material products of architecture, the focus of much writing in the field, reveal little about forms of underlying professional life and how they are changing.[31]

Today's powerful computing systems represent the latest in a series of technologies that practitioners have adopted, sometimes reluctantly, as a means of further defining both their professional relationships and their approach to architecture. Practitioners have long known that creating a place for themselves within the professional world means negotiating relationships with new technologies and through them. The history of technologies for representation in architecture has been well documented by scholars, including Mario Carpo and Robin Evans, who both write about architecture's shift from geometry to numeracy in the last few centuries.[32] Numerical means of describing architecture have been adopted by designers who have sought a generative language to command and control the organization of work. In this sense, Arup is not unique. However, as I will show, its history presents many salient examples of concurrent changes in technology and professional culture.

The Engineer, the Architect, and the Computer

Despite their early ambivalence, members of Arup have leveraged computer simulations in the dramatic transformation of their firm. In 1946, Ove Arup (1895–1988) founded the company as a one-person structural engineering consultancy in London. Today, Arup is a 10,000-person global partnership involved in at least 19 different architecture specializations and numerous other areas of design. From their shaping of the celebrated concrete shell structure at the Opera House in Sydney to their more recent predictions for the acoustics of the Lincoln Center renovation in New York City, practitioners at Arup have used innovations in computer simulation to challenge the discourse in architecture and articulate new possibilities for the field. These innovations have not only led to new designs. Arup has used simulations to reframe what architecture can do and this has expanded their domain of practice.

I return to Arup's work throughout this book because it exemplifies the symbiotic collaborative and competitive dynamics of contemporary practice in architecture. At the symposium of 1963, the discussion touched upon the implications of computing for professional relationships between the firm and its collaborators, particularly architects. Since the inception of Arup, being an engineer has meant negotiating a professional role in relationship to architects. In his speeches and writings, Ove Arup frequently juxtaposes the aims of the two disciplines.

> The reason for the difference between the architectural and engineering 'climate', so to speak, is very complex. It is partly a matter of terminology, partly a matter of historical accident, and the consequent training of architects and engineers, and mostly a matter of what is commonly supposed to be the difference in content or context – architecture being concerned with producing works of art; engineering with utility structures.[33]

In such remarks, Ove Arup is attentive to the complex history of interactions between architects and engineers. However, the extreme variability of those relationships can be further highlighted to show how the two disciplines help mutually to establish the legitimacy of one another. Engineers have maintained a place within architecture because of their ability to empower architects, even while taking an increasing amount of control off architects' hands. At the symposium, some engineers saw the computer as a threat to their relationships with architects, their primary collaborators, and thus a danger to their own professional positions. Indeed, the computer did come to change relationships in architecture, but not in ways that were easily predictable.

The juxtaposition of architects, engineers, and computers presented a complicated set of professional dynamics for symposium attendees to disentangle. Some attendees were already on the defense. One engineer reassured the group that "the computer couldn't really take the act of designing away from the architect . . . the essential thing to remember was that a computer didn't possess an imagination."[34] Other attendees looked forward to new empowering relationships between the three. One participant suggested that computers could expand the imagination of designers: "A computer ought to give the architect more choice, rather than simply produce an optimum solution for him."[35] At this early event, there were already intimations of a change in the way engineers and architects would work together. Professional dynamics and decisions would have to develop out of a tension between not two players, but three: the engineer, the architect, and the computer. In ensuing years, the number of participants in architecture has only multiplied.

Social Lives of Simulations

The Arup symposium primarily focused on the number-crunching capacity of computers. In the decades since 1963, designers have come to see computers less as calculating devices and more as simulation tools. This book will focus primarily on the use of computers to simulate the performance of buildings.

This is part of a broader trend in how we use computers for a range of activities. "We are moving towards a culture of simulation," writes sociologist and psychologist Sherry Turkle, "in which people are increasingly comfortable with substituting representations of reality for the real."[36] Turkle explores how living in virtual worlds affects the way we think about ourselves as well as what it means to be human.[37] However, her gaze does not often extend into the contemporary workplace. Here, I focus on how changes in technology are playing out in professional lives in architecture. In emerging cultures of computer simulation, practitioners characterize their work and themselves in novel ways. They use simulations to define new roles and relationships, to supplement traditional prescriptive ways of knowing, to overturn long-standing building regulations, and to delineate an extended range of acceptable forms. They harness their skills with simulations to expand into new areas of work and challenge traditional professional boundaries.

Designers use simulations in order to connect to materials and audiences in new ways. They aspire to new positions of creativity and control. However, simulations can also inspire the illusion that designers can become highly specialized while still maintaining a presence at the center of things. Consistent with what Turkle has found in personal lives, computers in professional lives are giving rise to new kinds of connectivity, but also increased isolation.[38] Specialist engineers and technical architects are connecting through technology by putting it at the center. Some of these practitioners are giving up their claims to generalized knowledge and establishing themselves on islands of expertise.[39] Designers are more connected than ever, but the strength of those connections and the effectiveness of the resulting network need to be put in question.[40] What do computer simulations take out of human hands, even as they connect designers to vast networks of resources otherwise out of reach?[41] In this context, we should reconsider what it means to be a designer in architecture by asking: what are the social and technological circumstances in which contemporary practitioners reflect on existing conditions and imagine alternatives?

An Ethnographic Account

I bring an interdisciplinary background to the study of changing relationships among humans, machines, and environments. As an ethnographer, a technologist, and a designer myself, I reflect on how practitioners in architecture see computer simulations from the perspective of a trained observer, a technology developer, and a participant.[42] Since I initiated this line of research 10 years ago, I have followed the stories of countless designers. I have conducted formal interviews with over 100 individuals. However, I find that presenting a few salient stories is the most effective way of illustrating how designers define themselves in this technological moment.[43]

My accounts of individual engineers and architects come primarily from fieldwork in a variety of American and British practices. However, the studies I conducted at the offices of Arup are in many ways at the heart of this book. Although it is not my intention to present a full profile of this or any firm, stories from individuals at Arup launch many of my discussions about what is happening more generally in architecture. This is only possible because Arup's extensive portfolio has made it a common denominator on projects around the world. It is one of a handful of large design consulting firms, including Buro Happold, for example, that provide the technical expertise behind many of the contemporary technological innovations in architecture.

My emphasis is on the diverse experiences of individuals in their organizational environs. At Arup in particular, accounts represent perspectives from many personal and professional backgrounds, generations, countries, and disciplines. From within Arup, I can observe different kinds of designers in close proximity. My intention in this book is to present salient accounts of changing design practices, to generate new discussions, and to discover important questions about the role of computer simulations in professional life, not to give an overview of changes across the field of architecture.

My empirical approach can be situated within a broad realm of qualitative research called ethnography, developed by anthropologists to study social groups through "thick" descriptions of their narrative and material cultures. Historically, ethnography has been used by western social scientists to learn about marginal or non-western cultures.[44] However, new generations of anthropologists are "studying up" in scientific and engineering laboratories.[45] Social scientists who study up have strayed from traditional ethnographies of peripheral cultures in order to examine institutions of power and social control.[46] New studies scrutinize the social structure of professional life to uncover the production of institutionalized knowledge and the way that experts persuade both the general public and policy makers. In recent years, multi-site ethnographies have tried to grapple with the increasingly distributed nature of contemporary technical and scientific cultures. My book deals with multiple sites and integrates a range of disciplinary perspectives because of the frayed boundaries of the practices I study. However, this work should not be mistaken for a global, or even a national, account of practices in architecture. Rather, I focus on a few targeted examples. These may seem foreign to designers who work under different social and technological circumstances. However, I believe that the stories presented in this book are illustrative of new and important professional dynamics developing along with computer simulations. The narratives of practitioners at Arup and other technologically advanced firms are lenses through which we can examine emerging conceptions of architecture and consider their implications.

Navigating this Book

This book is organized around the accounts of professional designers engaged in a high-stakes competition to redefine architecture in the context of computer simulation. Designers of a range of architectural systems, including facades, acoustical treatments, mechanical systems, and fire safety measures are challenging traditional practices in order to accommodate increasingly sophisticated simulation tools as well as new professional spaces for themselves.

In Chapter 2, I situate this study in a history of inquiry into the relationship between technology and professional culture. Computer simulation is often about professional jurisdiction, how work is controlled and distributed. Designers adopt computer simulations to expand their professional spaces. However, simulations are devices of communication; they only open opportunities for their operators if they appeal to the necessary audiences. Thus, simulations must be both technically defensible and culturally palatable. They are successful when they create what I am calling shared spaces of alternatives – literal and conceptual arenas in which participants in architecture can converge on design solutions, even if they have different personal and professional goals. These spaces of simulation make room for more profound professional transformations.

I draw upon my ethnographic fieldwork in order to explore key transformations in detail: the production of professional identity, the performance of expert knowledge, and the measure of good form. Chapters 3, 4, and 5 follow a two-part structure, starting with an episode from an office of generalist architects that introduces one of these transformational themes. Thereafter, each chapter delves into specialized domains, such as acoustics, fire safety, and structures, in order to explore its theme across different kinds of practice.

In Chapter 3, I consider how computer simulations shape new roles and relationships in architecture. Designers are working between worlds, in order both to adopt new technologies and retain traditional disciplinary allegiances. A master architect keeps a hand in design by staying close to his apprentice who is an architect, but also a hacker. An acoustician creates a dual identity as a scientist and a collaborative co-designer by opening acoustical analysis to simulated experience. A structural engineer communicates with hand drawing and the language of architects, but checks his work with advanced simulations. A fire safety engineer helps architects meet regulations, but uses simulations to get around them when the rules over-constrain their designs. The professional lives of these individuals illustrate new hybrid ways of being a designer that are developing around computer simulation.

I explore the way computer simulations work within social systems of knowledge in Chapter 4. Across a variety of specialized domains, simulations are put to test in consistent ways. First, simulations must produce results that are expected; they are limited by the intuitive understanding of their operators. Second, the uncertainties of simulations must be made explicit. Third, their results must be reconciled with complementary and competing representations. Finally, simulations must contend with traditional conceptions of knowledge, such as regulations and best practices. Simulations are never simply true. However, they can become trusted by an audience when framed in the right way.

In Chapter 5, I investigate how simulations support divergent notions of good form. Discourses on form often differentiate between the abstract idea behind a design and its concrete experience. In other words, form can be intent or performance. Often it is the intent that is attributed to architects, and the performance which is handled by engineers. Thus, engineers are gaining professional ground by using computer simulations to reframe architectural experience and how to create it. Engineers, architects, and other participants in design must reconcile their different perspectives on form. They do so in shared spaces of alternatives, arenas in which different representations of architecture can be exchanged, without the same understanding of the exchange. This book presents a pluralistic approach to form that acknowledges these shared spaces, gives legitimacy to all participating perspectives, and encourages more nuanced and responsible architectural results.

Next, in Chapter 6, I reflect on the structure of professional narratives themselves: their attributes and limits as tools of research. This book focuses on a limited set of narratives: those that speak to the themes of identity, knowledge, and form; those that fit well within particular genres (technical, analytical, methodological, reflective, and cultural); and those that expose new discourses developing around computer simulations. Listening to architecture, rather than simply looking at it, is a step toward a pluralistic formalism, in which multiple conflicting stories about design can be acknowledged and better supported by both researchers and developers of technology. In this context, narratives can be defined in political terms, by their transparency and their accessibility to reflection and critique. Finally, I also consider the way that metaphors of the theater pervade professional narratives about computer simulation. Probing these metaphors can reveal how creating a valid simulation, like creating a successful theater performance, depends upon connecting with audiences in the right way.

The book ends in Chapter 7 with a consideration of how professional narratives in architecture can be placed in the context of a broader set of accounts about how computer simulation is shaping relationships in many human–machine–environment interactions. The other half of this story in architecture, still untold, would require an exploration of the narratives of inhabitants. Professionals and inhabitants co-construct conceptions of architecture in buildings, neighborhoods, and cities. Expanding the scope of this research can reveal changing notions of human presence at many scales. Such studies would illuminate new *environmental imaginations*, the social and technological processes that shape our sense of place.

Chapter 2

Cultures of Simulation

Architecture has always been a culture of simulation. In fifteenth-century Italy, Filippo Brunelleschi invented linear perspective to simulate the visual perception of space.[47] In eighteenth-century France, Pierre Patte graphically mapped the propagation of sound in buildings.[48] A nineteenth-century architect from Spain, Antoni Gaudi, adopted a method called graphic statics to draw structural forces.[49] For many centuries, geometry was the medium of simulation.[50] By the twentieth century, numerical methods overtook graphical means in all these domains: lighting, acoustics, and structures.[51] Today's computer simulations extend numerical methods and through virtual reality connect the numbers to experience as never before. Although the media have changed, designers have always needed to inhabit their buildings virtually before they were built.

Thus, simulations are primary in architecture; they precede building. However, the uses of simulation are largely invisible to those outside the profession. Living in a building reveals little about designers' ways of working and thinking. By examining attitudes toward simulation in practice, we can learn much about changing professional conceptions of architecture: what it can do, how it can be done, and who can do it.

Contemporary designers are adopting computer simulations without necessarily giving up all their traditional methods. They generate and share design options through computer simulations of buildings as well as hand sketches and physical models. They analyze designs using computational measures of building performance as well as material experiments. They develop professional experience and intuition through virtual reality as well as through experiences of real buildings. While older methods of representing buildings have not disappeared, they have been swept up in new cultures. Early studies of computers in architecture describe practitioners who are focused on an opposition between digital and pre-digital methods.[52] Although we might try to conceptually undo this duality, we should be attentive to the way architecture is still framed by its practitioners in terms of this choice, for the selection of representations has implications for who is in control.

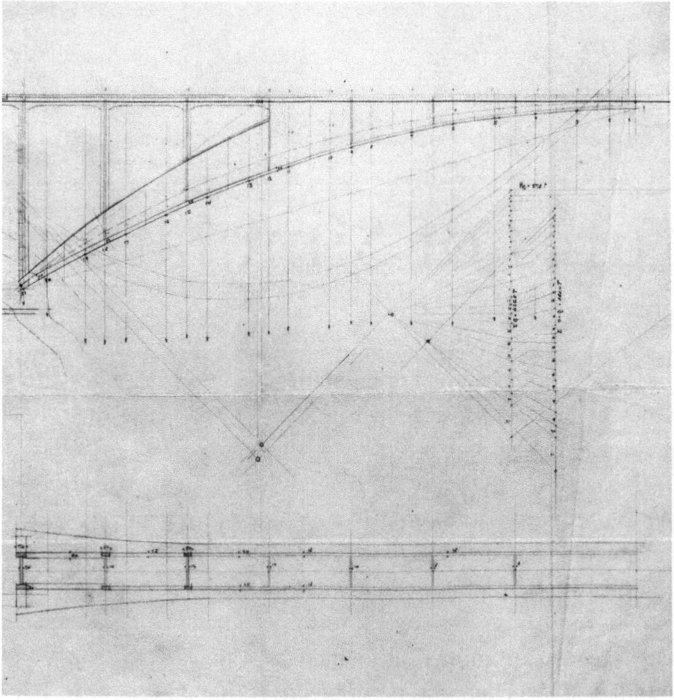

Figure 3
An example of graphic statics, a geometric approach to structural design, in a drawing by Robert Maillart for the Salginatobel Bridge, from the Maillart Archives, Eidgenössische Technische Hochschule (ETH), Zürich.

Architecture in Flux

"Why do we have to change? We've been building buildings for years without CATIA?" Roger Norfleet, a practicing architect in his thirties, poses this question to Tim Quix, an engineer and a generation older. Quix is an expert in CATIA, a digital design tool developed by Dassault Systèmes in the early 1980s for use by aerospace engineers.[53] It is 2005 and CATIA has just come into use at Paul Morris Associates, the 30-person architecture firm in the United States where Norfleet and Quix work. Each of them struggles with what it will mean for them, their firm, and their respective professions. New technologies for design are about creativity, but also about jurisdiction, about who controls the design process.

Architectural theorist Dana Cuff writes that each generation of architects is educated to understand what constitutes a creative act, and who in the system of their profession is empowered to use it and at what point.[54] Creativity is socially constructed and Norfleet is coming of age as an architect at a time of technological but also social transition. He must come to terms with the increasingly complex simulation tools that have changed both creativity and the rules by which it can operate.

Historically, architecture has been defined by its practitioners and patrons in relation to a diverse set of standards: technical, economic, and aesthetic. Buildings must be sound, practical, and beautiful. Vitruvius, author of one of the earliest known architectural treatises, *De Architectura*, expressed these qualities in Latin as *firmitas*, *utilitas*, and *venustas*. Modern architects have maintained distance from technical and economic activities in order to privilege their aesthetic role, what the sociologist Magali Sarfatti Larson has called the "aesthetics of construction."[55] However, with new technologies for simulation, embodied by programs such as CATIA, things are changing: new forms of technical expertise are becoming central to negotiations of jurisdiction in architecture.

In today's practices, in 2012, architects use software to produce three-dimensional geometric models. Sometimes they use off-the-shelf commercial software like CATIA, sometimes they customize this software through plug-ins and scripts, sometimes they work with software that they themselves have programmed. And yet, conforming to Larson's ideas that they claim the higher ground by identifying with art and not with science, contemporary architects do not often use the term "simulation." For some, it carries the connotation of a staged representation of reality. Rather, architects have held onto traditional terms such as "modeling" to distinguish their practices with digital technology. In fact, modeling can refer to more open-ended ways of applying the same technologies. Architect Daniel Cardoso explains: "there's something nice about the word modeling, which suggests handcraft, the shaping of objects, and the contact with a material, which simulation just doesn't have."[56] But whether or not they use the term, these technologies are creating new architectural identities and transforming relationships among a range of collaborators: masters and apprentices, students and teachers, architects and engineers. These days, constructing an identity in architecture requires that one define oneself in relation to simulation.[57]

Engineers differ from architects in their attitudes toward computer simulation. They work with simulation software that allows deep technical customization, and thus they can be dismissive of the less technical versions which architects use. Engineers identify with the science behind the technology and are more likely to cultivate relationships with academic, governmental, and commercial institutions that develop simulations. They also have a more collaborative outlook: as consultants, their primary focus is on developing simulations to satisfy professional relationships with clients, colleagues, and regulators. Architects face this problem as well, but to a lesser degree.

Both architects and engineers expect technologies to expand their professional roles. While some architects are seeking out more technical identities, engineers are looking for opportunities to be creative and to be involved earlier in the design process. Throughout the book, I will examine both sides of this transformation. However, my emphasis is on the evolving technical capabilities of designers rather than on the aesthetic explorations that have also accompanied the increased use of computer simulation. In order to discuss emerging cultures of computer simulation in architecture, we must first define our terms. What is a simulation? What does it mean for professionals to define themselves in relation to computer simulation?

The Difficulty of Defining Simulation

The term "simulation" has a circuitous history. It can be traced to the Middle Ages, when it was used to identify a practice or object that imitates for the purpose of deception.[58] With the invention of systems engineering and computers in the twentieth century, the term has been appropriated for more practical applications.[59] However, for scholars in the humanities, including some who are important to architects, simulation still retains the suggestion of illusion or even seduction.[60] In science and engineering, simulations are techniques and apparatuses designed to imitate actual processes for the production of knowledge. Simulations are a means of extrapolating from what we already know. For example, as Herbert Simon explains, simulation might be used as a technique for "deriving, from our knowledge of mechanisms governing the behavior of gases, a theory of the weather and a means of weather prediction."[61]

In an architectural context, simulations replicate some of the conditions of built environments, including material behaviors and perceptual phenomena, for purposes ranging from creative exploration to public explanation. This book focuses on simulations that are constructed on computers, but which have many possible outputs (numerical, visual, aural, etc.) In my discussions, the term simulation can refer to the mechanism itself (computer hardware and software), or its results, just as the term drawing can signify both the process and the product of making marks on paper. Through digital control over interactive media, simulations can create dynamic, responsive, and even immersive imitations of architecture. Recent computer simulations do not simply illustrate building physics; they use virtual reality to demonstrate the implications for human beings.

Although computer simulations share a common digital platform, they vary widely in their application and construction. We may differentiate computer simulations according to their underlying methods. Finite element analysis and ray tracing are different methods of computer simulation, each with countless algorithmic variations. Simulations also differ in terms of their interfaces. They may draw you into their world or offer a god's eye view. Simulations may be categorized by the conditions they are used to imitate, such as lighting, acoustics, or structural forces. They can also be classified as explanatory tools or tools for exploration, meaning they either suggest new possibilities or convey what their users already know. The term simulation in today's practices does not signify a singular or an isolated process.

Simulations are part of a broad system of knowledge, composed of theories, material processes, mathematical artifacts, and interpretations. They occupy an uncertain place between better established areas of practice. In science, simulations resist categorization into the traditional practices of theory and experimentation. Simulations are hybrids; they combine different ways of knowing.[62] Furthermore, each simulation is a semiotic system and has uncertain interpretations. Simulations are given meaning in context. In this sense, they only produce knowledge in the hands of expert users.

Given the broad range of implementations and uses, computer simulations resist easy assimilation into a taxonomy of representations, by which I mean a complete classification of the descriptive mechanisms that practitioners use. In *The Sciences of the Artificial*, Simon calls for just such a taxonomy as an essential component in the development of his "science of design."[63] Here, I grapple with the problems inherent in classifying computer simulations. I believe that we may come closer to an understanding of simulations and their role in architecture by eschewing the search for a static definition. Simulations are betwixt and between; their characteristics are defined by the worlds they connect.[64]

I believe, along with philosophers of science and technology, Sergio Sismondo and Eric Winsberg, that "simulation" does not have a fixed definition or meaning, any more than "architecture" does.[65] What differentiates simulations from other representations used in architecture, including models, visualizations, and abstractions? Many practitioners say that they do not have an answer to this question, either because these terms are interchangeable, or because the distinctions are simply not apparent outside the context of use. However, this does not mean that attempts by practitioners to distinguish simulation from other techniques are not important. The term simulation has a rhetorical significance in such explanations. It is a frame through which practitioners reflect on the technical and cultural changes in their work and make new ideological and competitive assertions about what it means to do architecture and to be a designer. By giving attention to the ways in which practitioners search in an open-ended way for the meaning of simulation, I am treating the term ethnographically.[66]

The Shared Space of Alternatives

To "profess" once meant "to take a vow of faith." It was a clerical ritual.[67] During the rise to power of professionals in the nineteenth century, this vow was secularized. The profession of faith was transformed into a profession of knowledge. Today, professionals claim specialized knowledge as a means of identifying their place as part of a social system.[68] Émile Durkheim helped to prefigure a systems view of professions when he wrote about these groups as the "organs of society," only partly autonomous entities that cannot exist except in contact with one another.[69] More recently, Andrew Abbott has elaborated our understanding of professional systems, writing about how "tasks, professions, and links between them change continuously."[70] For Abbott, professions make up an interdependent system in which jurisdictional boundaries are perpetually in dispute.

In my study of architecture and simulation, I adopt Abbott's view that jurisdiction is the defining relation between professionals. However, I propose that it is negotiated not just through competition, as Abbott claims, but through symbiotic collaboration as well. Professionals must define their work in relationship to outsiders who challenge their control over specific areas of knowledge. They define problems and defend against competing definitions in a continual cycle of self-invention. Designers have always used technology to define their problems and themselves.[71] This is not new. Every technology shapes conceptions of architecture. By tracking changes in the way architecture is defined, we can see how professional positions and positions toward technology co-evolve.

For instance, computer simulations are often created to meet the specific needs of clients and collaborators. This is to say that professionals often develop simulations and relationships in tandem. Sometimes the two become linked so closely that they are difficult to disentangle. Clients come to expect certain simulations; they become comfortable with "their" technologies, independently of what the project merits from a technical perspective.

With the creation of each simulation, professionals must ask themselves, "What type of relationship will this satisfy and for what end?" The success of any simulation depends on its fit with an audience. Simulations must be technically defensible, but also culturally palatable. On each project and with each new client, professionals must learn how to use simulations to engage an audience on their own terms. One way of acknowledging how simulations enable successful interactions among professionals, clients, collaborators, and regulators is to look at these technologies as "trading zones."[72] In *Image and Logic*, historian of science Peter Galison explains how pidgin languages are used to communicate across social and epistemological boundaries. On Galison's account, different social groups can productively "trade" objects and information without having the same understanding of the exchange. Galison is not an ethnographer, but he adopts an ethnographic lens when he sees simulations as trading zones in the work of microphysicists. He writes that simulations have been "arenas in which radically different activities could be locally, but not globally coordinated."[73]

Although the concept of the trade is not widely used in architecture, engaging the metaphor of a space – what Galison calls a "zone" – to describe a range of possible outcomes is common. Herbert Simon uses the notion of a "space of alternatives" to describe the bounded set of possibilities in which designers "search" for an outcome that "satisfices."[74] This hybrid term is one of Simon's neologisms, combining aspects of satisfying and sufficing. Simon's use of a spatial metaphor to describe a set of designs suggests that there are techniques by which designers can find good designs, if they look in the right places. His writing extends a metaphor that has long held the attention of architects who believe that design is exploration.[75] For example, Frank Lloyd Wright wrote "in the stony bonework of the Earth . . . there sleep forms and styles enough for all ages, for all of Man."[76] For Wright, nature held the space of alternatives. For Simon, the space of alternatives is a computational space. By expanding the discussion of design as exploration to include reference to Galison's trading zone, we acknowledge that design spaces are collaborative and that we should allow for multiple meanings to adhere. A successful design space is one in which many people can coordinate ideas and contribute to designs without necessarily understanding too deeply the perspectives of all other participants.

Thus we can enrich Simon's notion of the space of design alternatives by seeing it with an ethnographic or social lens. In this sense, simulations in architecture can be seen as shared, yet participant-specific, spaces of exploration. Designers use simulations to shape spaces of alternatives with clients, collaborators, and regulators. In the chapters that follow, I will illustrate how computer simulations shape new spaces for design – literal and conceptual arenas in which professionals and their publics can explore new identities, knowledge, and design outcomes in parallel.

Beyond Instrumentality

Information technologies for simulation have been hailed by practitioners and academics alike as offering new solutions to technical problems: they simplify the construction of complex curved surfaces and bring invisible phenomena, like acoustics and airflow, into view.[77] It is not difficult to see simulations as powerful instruments in the hands of professionals, but this widespread perspective can be enriched by considering how instruments shape our thinking about our work and ourselves.

In "The Question Concerning Technology," Heidegger warns against taking technologies at their instrumental value.[78] For Heidegger, technologies do not simply allow us to act on the world; they reveal the world to us in particular ways. Revealing is at the root of technology's apparent instrumentality. As an example, Heidegger asks us to think of a tract of land transformed in the hauling out of coal and ore. Here, the earth is revealed as a coal-mining district and the soil as a mineral deposit. The field that the peasant formerly cultivated and set in order appears different through the framing of technology. In this way, cautions Heidegger, technologies can overshadow and obscure other, and perhaps more holistic, ways of representing nature.

Although the illusion of instrumentality is of concern, Heidegger's view should be tempered. Technologies reveal different things for different people. Sherry Turkle and educational pioneer Seymour Papert work together to explain new pluralisms, in which "different people make computers their own in their own way."[79] With simulations at hand and in mind, practitioners are defining a variety of new practices and embracing a range of new conceptions about architecture. So when we look at simulations, we should be aware of how they frame our worlds. But we should also resist the temptation to see them as deterministic. The diversity of new practices emerging in architecture suggests that simulations enable not fewer, but more ways of seeing.

Let us consider another perspective on the relationship between technology and professional work. In *The Reflective Practitioner*, theorist Donald Schön defines design as "a conversation with the materials of the situation."[80] This is true in a deeper sense than Schön suggests. It is true not only of the design process, Schön's interest, but of the conceptualization of design as a domain of work. Design does not simply happen within a noteworthy social and technological context; design cannot be extracted from this context. The meaning and goals of design emerge only in a conversation with the materials of the situation. The dynamics of this conversation in contemporary practice cannot be explained without an understanding of computer simulations.

The instrumental view of simulations has been questioned widely in social studies of technology. In Galison's work, we can see how the development of computer simulations challenged the professional identity of microphysicists. In *Image and Logic*, he explains the fight for legitimacy waged by the operators of simulations:

> As they struggled to find a place in the traditional categories of experiment and theory, the simulators both altered and helped define what it meant to be an experimenter or a theorist in the decades following World War II.[81]

Galison's work elucidates the social implications of adopting new technologies in professional worlds. Simulations shape new roles and relationships. They have profound implications for the production of work, knowledge, and professional identity. However, like any technology, simulations are in turn shaped by a social context. After all, we make our simulations. In "Models, Simulations, and Their Objects," philosopher of science Sergio Sismondo explains how the instrumental view obscures the social shaping of technologies.[82] He writes that simulations:

> are created to fit into particular cultures of research: models and simulations have to take particular forms in order to be accepted. And they are created to fit into particular social settings, becoming objective by balancing among sides in debates.[83]

Simulations both define and are defined by the professional work of which they are a part. If we are to understand new forms of professional life in the domain of architecture, we must examine simulations beyond their instrumental value.

Biography of a Simulation

Let's look at how simulations shape and are shaped by the social organization of professional work in architecture by considering the case of Fablon. This is one of many computer simulations, originally developed and refined by a string of individuals at Arup to address specific projects; retooled by various researchers, designers, and programmers; and conditioned by the constraints of new assumptions, audiences, and supporting technologies. In its current form, Fablon has become standard software at Arup. Although its history illustrates the social construction of a technology, the story of Fablon also reveals how simulations can reciprocally inform the organization of work, connecting practitioners in ways that challenge old spatial and temporal divisions of labor.[84]

Fablon is a structural simulator based on the theory of dynamic relaxation, a general method of non-linear analysis that relies on an iterative approach to resolve the relationships among a number of independently defined elements. Dynamic relaxation was initially adopted at Arup in the 1970s by Alistair Day as a technique for form-finding in cable and fabric structures.[85] An early version of Fablon took input from text files, each consisting of a list of coordinates for nodes and connecting elements, such as bars or cables, and parameters for those elements.[86] However, this interface made Fablon difficult to use for design. Text files, essentially long lists of x, y, and z values, had to be manually assembled for each design option. Testing a number of options was difficult and time consuming.

Fablon and other early simulations at Arup brought with them new routines and timescales, but also new assumptions about the relationship between practice and scientific theory. In order to understand some of the changes in thinking that Fablon heralded in the design of architectural structures, it is important to consider its epistemological underpinnings. Fablon, like all computer simulations, relies on discretization, the process by which simulations convert differential equations, which express rates of change over continuous intervals, into difference equations, which express rates of change over discrete or finite intervals.[87] Digital computers can only handle discrete intervals of space and time. Thus, Fablon approximates the loads on a

Figure 4
Marsyas, a site-specific stretched-fabric installation by Anish Kapoor in collaboration with Arup at the Tate Modern gallery in London.

cable or fabric structure by discretizing them into nodes, rather than representing the continuous distribution of loads such as gravity over the entire interval of the structure. At every level of their design, computers are made to represent the world in finite states. From the binary level, where computers manage only values of 0 or 1, to the display of visual information in the form of pixels, computers are based on a philosophy of discretization. By computing one finite state at a time, computer simulations can solve otherwise intractable numerical problems. This is a great strength, but also a serious limitation.[88]

As Winsberg explains, discretization is fundamental to the new epistemology of computer simulation.[89] In particular, the finite techniques of

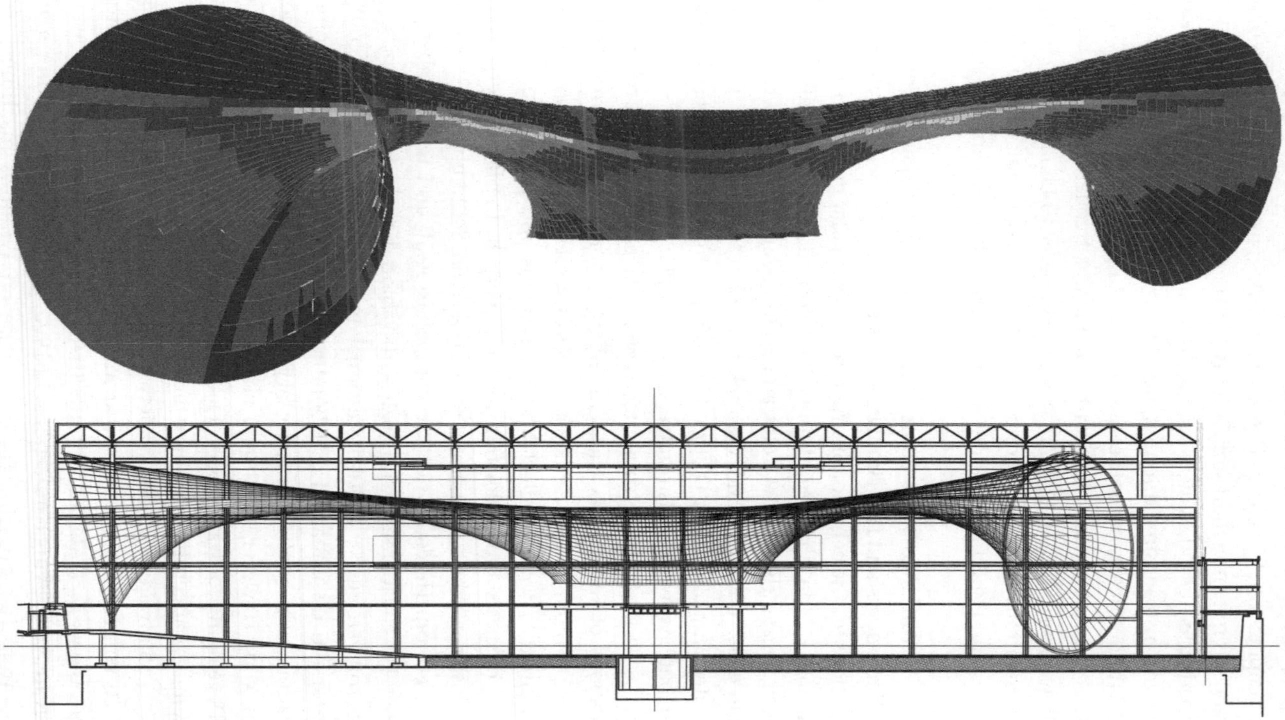

Figure 5
A simulation of structural forces in *Marsyas* generated using Fablon.

simulation have led to loose relationships between practice and theory. This is because simulationists, Winsberg's term for practitioners of simulation, often cannot discretize their models in the principled way suggested by theory. Therefore, they look for ways to make the models simpler, which requires inventions and deviations from the theory. Simulationists do this by electing to use a computationally "cheaper" solution.[90] Often, just lowering the resolution of a model is not enough. If simulationists lower the resolution too much, they may inadvertently hide salient features that are important to the behavior of the system. Instead, simulationists introduce compensation factors that do not arise from the theory, but rather are designed to produce the kind of expected effects of the system. In other words, simulations frequently are not designed to follow theory. Rather, they are designed in order to behave in an expected way. Simulations are judged primarily by looking at the relationship between outcomes and expectations, not by scrutinizing their premises or underlying theory.

I will discuss this point in more depth in Chapter 4. For now, it is enough to understand that simulations are tweaked by their operators to meet expectations for the behavior of structures on particular projects. The computer simulation Fablon emerged through the conditions of a number of Arup projects. It gave rise to new roles and relationships – between theorists and programmers, designers and toolmakers, and researchers and practitioners. Computer simulations like Fablon shape not just how loads are distributed in a model, but how work is distributed among people.

Various projects supported Fablon's development. One of the earliest applications of Fablon was the Schlumberger fabric structure in Cambridge, UK. The pavilion, which resembles a series of suspension bridges, was designed in conjunction with architect Michael Hopkins and completed in 1992. A network of masts and cables transmits the loads in the fabric to the ground. Brian Foster, a fabric expert at Arup, worked on Schlumberger, but did not operate Fablon. He could not use computers at all and is remembered as a designer. His collaborator, who dealt with Fablon directly, is remembered only as "the software guy."[91] These professional dynamics, with Foster designing the structure and his unnamed collaborator designing the supporting computer simulation, were perhaps a necessary but often overlooked distribution of design work. However, we should not underestimate the importance of each role. Developing software is part of architecture design when decisions made by programmers affect the forms in which building inhabitants must dwell.

Software enables a variety of new relationships in design. Fablon connects contemporary designers at Arup to engineers from Arup's history. It extends the work of Alistair Day and Brian Foster into the present. However, it also creates new, living connections. In 1995, Pierre Moreau, a young engineer, joined Arup. He converted Fablon for use on Windows machines. Moreau works with Arup's Advanced Geometry Unit, where projects are emphatically collaborative. He explains that the engineers of the Advanced Geometry Unit, as well as their collaborating architects, all have their hands in the design.

> We tend to be more hands on with projects. We use automation techniques to go back and forth, adding and subtracting elements until the design works. [It is an] iterative kind of optimization. It allows you to deal with complex forms. You get rid of the bottleneck of analysis. Previously, it might take you a month to run the analysis, now there is a potential to do some analysis in real time or close to it.[92]

The simulations used in the Advanced Geometry Unit allow different participants to feel connected to the design in their own way. In empowering their clients and collaborators, the software makes present the work of the engineers who design and operate it. "This allows the designer to go forward," says Moreau. "It offers new freedom to be expressive."

In 1998, Moreau rewrote Fablon over the course of three weeks for use on Jusco, a project in Tokyo. This time, there was no architect on the project. A contractor designed the majority of the building and Arup was hired to resolve the problem of the fabric roof. When Moreau started on the job, the lead Arup engineer was making do with a crude physical model made of balsa wood and tights. Later, Moreau used Fablon to help the artist Anish Kapoor design *Marsyas*, a grandiose stretched-fabric structure for the Tate Modern gallery in London (see Figures 4 and 5). Moreau has created a place for himself through his work on Fablon. He and other programmers at Arup have become catalysts for new explorations of form, but often, the programmers do not introduce themselves as designers. Moreau sees his role as supportive rather than expressive. When he talks about a new freedom for designers, he is speaking about opportunities for "architects and artists." Although Moreau is "hands on" in his own way, his role is mediated. He participates in design, but does not call himself a designer. I threaten such subtle distinctions when I use the unqualified term, designer, to describe Moreau and his colleagues. However, I do so in order to challenge nascent attributions of authorship in new human–machine configurations.

When Moreau revived the Fablon code for use on his Windows computer, he was the only user. Only recently has the program attracted enough attention to make it worth broad support by Oasys, the software engineering branch of Arup. Hans Dyson, a programmer at Oasys, has taken on the task of distributing Fablon more widely, by integrating it to GSA, the home-brewed, general structural analysis tool used throughout Arup's many offices. Dyson wrote a wrapper that allows Fablon to communicate with GSA. This process has taken four years and, to Moreau's dismay, has resulted in a more limited version of the simulation. "Bits of the original Fablon have been taken out and the whole program has been dumbed down," laments Moreau; however, he concedes that most of the elements taken out were not likely to be used. The GSA version of Fablon is functional, but it has been transformed into something Moreau no longer recognizes or controls. It is an evolution of the simulation, but it brings a sense of loss. The primary benefit of Dyson's work on Fablon has been a visual graphic interface, as a result of its integration with GSA. The implications, says Moreau, are that you no longer have to be a "super-specialist" to use it. In this sense, Fablon is becoming less personal but more connective than ever.

Fablon's development, first through individual projects, then later through its integration into Arup's general structural modeling platform is not necessarily typical. Frequently, the simulations used at Arup were developed elsewhere, in independent software engineering firms or in non-profit building technology research laboratories run by governments or universities. However, all simulations have development trajectories that are shaped by, and help to shape, the social organization of work around them. They connect practitioners to voices and judgments from the past registered in computer code, and allow them to be "hands on" in a variety of mediated capacities. Simulations have a social place in practice. In fact, simulations draw their power from the way in which they are able to connect people, theories, experiences, and materials. They support new roles and relationships at either end of their development, for both programmers and operators.

Designers as Toolmakers

> Writing programmes for a computer is rather like learning to speak a foreign language . . . A few stumbling sentences are permissible, but it is entirely another matter when it comes to attempting a novel. The conception, production and 'de-bugging' of a complex programme is a job for a fluent 'linguist' – not a civil engineer.[93]

With this quote, we return to Arup's 1963 "Symposium on the Use of Computers." At the time, most technically oriented designers conducted their analysis of buildings by hand. For these practitioners, programming was an opaque means of describing the world. It appeared to be foreign and tedious. They assumed that making good software would employ an alien form of expertise, not one appropriate for designers. Since then, programming has become a primary means of working for a growing number of architects and engineers. These practitioners have made writing code and the development of software their means of participating in design.

When I first started to look into programming practices at Arup, I assumed the firm was hiring programming specialists to write software. In an early meeting with Emmanuel West, a mechanical engineer by training, I explained that I was interested in learning about how programmers were becoming designers. "Software engineers aren't becoming designers," explained West. "It's the other way around." Contrary to what I expected, and what Arup symposium participants anticipated in 1963, software development is increasingly done by people with backgrounds in design. These designers have become design toolmakers, and many of them are self-taught. They have created new roles for themselves by embracing the language of the computer as an extension of the design discourse.

By the time of the Arup symposium, some practitioners had already caught on to the idea that engineers could create their own small programs to solve project-based problems. One participant is noted as saying, "But the use of a computer for small problems is another matter. In this case it is better for the engineer to write small programmes. And the distinction between small and large programmes is dependent on the experience of the engineer."[94] Today, many architects and engineers do develop their own programs. "You get lots of little pockets of development," says David Turner, member of Oasys, the group at Arup focused on the development of general use software packages. "Programming is becoming easier because it's taught in the universities," he explains. Designers are less likely to write code for the first time while on the job. Although Oasys turns out its own software, it also facilitates the augmentation of software by others at Arup, through methods like scripting, a simplified, end-user form of programming intended specifically for modifying or automating existing software.

Many times, designers adjust and update simulations in order to meet the requirements of clients. Patrick McCormack, one of the members of Oasys, describes this as "bending" and "tuning" the simulation to satisfy different needs.[95] "Some of them get it to sing," notes McCormack, but every designer who has used Fablon has contributed to the culture of programming at Arup. One of the consistent attitudes toward simulation at Arup has been that individuals should be given space and support to develop their own tools.[96] If someone has an idea, Oasys will help to carry it through; if the idea is generalizable, an application can be created and disseminated within the firm or beyond. Programming is by no means pervasive, but it is increasingly an acknowledged means by which Arup designers can connect to a wide range of people and projects. It is one level at which practices of simulation establish new relationships in architecture.

In order to encourage script writing, Turner and his team have developed common interfaces, enabling practitioners to automate native Arup applications such as the firm's general structural analysis program. "People see an opportunity to improve something. Sometimes those bits of development become major applications," says Turner. Programming is a way of building upon what has been done before and influencing what may come after. It is a connection with others who have written and will write code for the same software or simply employ it artfully.

And yet, it is not unusual for the difficulty of a programming project to defy the abilities of the typical designer. Some sentiments from the 1963 symposium still hold, including the notion that "it is a professional job to produce a useable programme and the larger and more complex the job, the more vital is professional help."[97] Arup's in-house software development groups such as Oasys and the Advanced Technology Group aid project-based practitioners in developing complex software.

One of the "core values" of Arup is the capability to solve any problem for the customer, no matter how difficult, says Barrett Chapman, a member of the Advanced Technology Group, who works out of a small Arup outpost in Birmingham, UK. Chapman had little computational training when he entered Arup, after studying general engineering in college. Over the course of 20 years, he has become a professional program designer. He explains his highly specialized role by saying, "I only get involved when the problems are really difficult, when there are no existing resources to solve the problem within Arup."[98]

David Turner at Oasys performs some of the same tasks as Chapman. For instance, he encountered an Arup designer who was painstakingly trying to work out the optimum seat racking on a stadium so that he could fit in as many people as possible, while allowing maximum visibility of the field for all. Turner first learned about the designer's problem by asking questions. "How do you work this out? What's your calculation?" Within a few days, they had built a rudimentary piece of software together. Turner describes how the simulation served the designer's goals: "You could put in the basic parameters and it would optimize that curve for him, showing every single tread and so on."[99]

When the expertise to do this programming is not on hand in project teams, practitioners like McCormack, Chapman, and Turner step in to help. Chapman and McCormack have backgrounds in engineering.[100] Turner was trained as a product designer. His perspective on this process is surprisingly self-effacing. "I'm more qualified to design a washing machine than I am to do anything with a building." Turner learned to program on his own, but explains that "a lot of people work that way. I'm not unique in that respect." His group creates new software through creative discussions with project teams. Converting design thinking into broadly applicable software is their niche, but they see this role in vastly different ways. Chapman explains it as "backroom" work. In contrast, McCormack has an empowered view of his role. He says that his work on graphics, interfaces, and manipulability can encourage more interrogation of what's behind the software and an increased sense of responsibility on the part of users to filter the results. As we have seen, programming is establishing new social roles and relationships in architecture, but not in deterministic ways. Designers see the development of simulations through their own personal and strategic lenses. Programming can bring a range of different things to practitioners.

In recent years, Oasys has become a financially independent business entity. The group earns money by selling software products both internally and externally. In a financial sense, Arup is now a customer for Oasys. However, decisions at Oasys are still directed by discussions within Arup. The work of Oasys is as much about developing a community at Arup as it is about independent economic success. For example, the transition from DOS to Windows at Oasys, says McCormack, was largely about preserving relationships within Arup. He explains the costs of not making the transition to Windows along with the rest of Arup in this way: "I had good relationships that I didn't want to give up. They had confidence in what we were doing. I didn't want to lose that."

In-house software development at Oasys offers Arup an opportunity to develop new simulations and to extend existing ones; a platform like GSA accommodates add-ons and refinements easily.[101] It also allows for some degree of quality control. Furthermore, software development is useful in a global organization because it offers the potential for virtual commonality through a shared platform. Given Arup's diverse network of offices, it would be impossible to have this commonality otherwise. Taking a look at their large markets, they would be using one system in the US, another in England, and yet another in Australia. Individual preferences would drive these choices, as would clients, regulations, and other local considerations. At many levels, from the personal to the organizational, building good software is about the relationships the software enables. "Simulations broaden the perspective of individuals," explains Alvin Bernard, who works on issues of knowledge management at Arup. "They reassure you. They say someone has done this before." The software developed by Oasys cannot easily be separated from the human connections that accompany it. One of the things that makes Arup's software so good, asserts McCormack, is the level of support that Oasys' employees put behind it. Even though there are only a handful of people in the office of Oasys, they spend a considerable amount of time helping project teams to realize specific goals. Software specialists enable broader cultures of simulation at Arup.

We can define expert cultures by their methods of representation, explains historian of science Evelyn Fox Keller.[102] Keller studies scientific practices in biology, but her terminology can be used to understand how designers at Arup define themselves in relationship to the simulations they employ. For Keller, the temporal, disciplinary, and culturally specific needs that must be satisfied by a representation are the characteristics that define an "epistemological culture."[103] These needs may be for prediction, control, or simply narrative coherence. They may be cognitive, instrumental, social, or psychological needs. Typically, the aim of any representation is to satisfy many needs at once.

When we apply this thinking to the stories from Arup, we can see code as an important representational medium that brings designers together in new ways. Programming connects people across disciplinary boundaries, through generations, and around the world. It has become a facet of professional identity and a means by which practitioners can position themselves within design. Hacking code has joined practices like publishing papers and projects as a culturally acceptable means of producing knowledge in architecture. Using, augmenting, and developing simulations are all means of participating in the life of a design office as well as a mechanism for reaching out to clients and an extended network of practitioners who share your software.

Inevitably, pitfalls accompany these new ways of relating. McCormack is wary that becoming too reliant on the chain of knowledge in simulations can become a form of dependence. He sees this as one of the main questions for Oasys: how can designers overcome the problems of increasing dependence on software? McCormack sees a willingness, especially on the part of younger designers, to ignore what's behind the software, the building physics. He laments that "in days gone by there was more vigilance." Similarly, Halden Harrison, a veteran structural engineer at Arup, fears that young engineers rely too much on the computer. He says that there is a dangerous assumption that if you can build it in the computer, then you can build it on site.[104] Particularly as simulations get larger and more sophisticated, there is an increasing need to understand what happens inside simulations in order to interpret them accurately.

These comments recall Turkle's distinction between two kinds of "transparency" in technological cultures.[105] Modernist transparency is the notion that users can and should have access to the inner workings of a technology. It evokes the aesthetic of early relationships with cars in which one could "open the hood and see inside."[106] This is the kind of relationship with simulation that Harrison and McCormack want for designers. "A good project engineer will know what to expect from a simulation," insists McCormack. Turkle contrasts this with an opposing, post-modern meaning of the term – the notion that something is transparent if you can use it without knowing how it works. Post-modern transparency allows the user to navigate the surface of a system without ever having to access its underlying mechanics. Are young engineers more susceptible to post-modern ways of seeing simulation? In defense against this possibility, McCormack argues that well-designed simulations, their graphics, interfaces, and manipulability, should encourage more interrogation of what is behind the software. Designers in cultures of computer simulation are in a struggle to find the best ways of using new technology both to expand their reach, but also to protect their core values. This is true for engineers as well as architects.

Designers as Operators

Let us momentarily move away from the engineering context and look at how simulation can both establish and hinder new relationships when appropriated in an office of architects. The following story takes us back into the world of practice at Paul Morris Associates, to reveal what architects see at stake in becoming operators of technology: nothing less than their creativity and their control over design.

In 2010, Paul Morris hired Tim Quix to teach architects at his firm how CATIA might be used to model designs rigorously in three dimensions. Although Quix was never trained in architecture, he has been working in the field for almost two decades. Quix once taught and sold CATIA to its intended users in the aerospace industry, working primarily as an employee of IBM, the parent company of Dassault Systèmes. Now, years later, Quix is using his expertise in CATIA to create a role for himself in architecture, a field he flirted with briefly as a young man, but turned away from to pursue his fascination with computer-aided design. Today, Quix is teaching CATIA at Paul Morris Associates and also working to apply the software to the firm's current projects. However, there is active resistance to his presence, for control over CATIA translates into a great deal of control indeed. Before designs are built, they only exist as representations; whoever models a project produces and controls the current reality of the design.

At Paul Morris Associates, this resistance to CATIA is shaped by many considerations. Rikle Shales, an architect in her mid-thirties, resists putting designs into CATIA because she says that once they are thus represented, people tend to see the designs as frozen, as a done deal. She points to the number of design changes that take place in an ongoing project and argues for keeping designs out of CATIA until late in the process. She says, "Quix has a habit of thinking that if we just put things into CATIA, they will be done and coordinated. It's pointless to model the current design in CATIA when it is almost certain to change."[107] Her position is well reasoned, but she and the architects around her know that it has a political dimension. Keeping designs off CATIA allows her to stay in greater control of the design process. Once designs are in CATIA, one might say that they all belong to Quix because he is the one best positioned to manipulate them.

Quix and his architect opponents define themselves in relation to CATIA and one another. From Quix's perspective, architecture needs CATIA, which can bring a new precision to building. He reasons that architects have difficulty learning CATIA because it requires a "level of rigor that architects are not used to." His colleagues' resistance to CATIA reinforces his sense of being different from those around him; he is the one who is a rigorous engineer.

Indeed, Quix describes his life at Paul Morris Associates in terms of "three difficult phases," each one a stage that includes some resistance to CATIA. He calls the first phase "the brick wall." In this phase, he says, architects complain that they are too busy to learn, that the program is foreign, and that it feels like somebody else's approach to architecture. Quix refers to this first phase as "a sickness called NIH (Not Invented Here)." In the brick-wall phase, Quix is isolated.

A second phase begins when Paul Morris, the founding principal of the firm, actually orders a team of architects to learn CATIA, with Quix as their tutor. Quix teaches the practitioners one by one. This second phase, in which CATIA is viewed very differently by the practitioners and their teacher, is "tutelage with resistance." Quix sees CATIA as a new way of looking at the world, a systematic and three-dimensional way of approaching design. Most centrally, for him it is a new way of being an architect. Quix feels he is bringing more than a new piece of software to Paul Morris Associates; rather, he feels he is bringing its architects a new epistemology and a new identity.

For the designers who are his students, CATIA is simply a technique, one more skill set to apply to their practical problems. The conflict between Quix and the architects of Paul Morris Associates calls to mind the concept of transparency once again. In this case, Quix favors transparency in the modernist sense; he seeks a deep understanding of CATIA. Meanwhile, the post-modern sensibility guides the understanding of technology that interests many of Quix's students.

Robert Laird, an architect, is someone whom Quix considers something of a protégé. Laird has mastered working on the "surface" of CATIA. Laird has been using three-dimensional modeling programs since his years as an undergraduate majoring in architecture: AutoCAD, 3D Studio Max, Rhinoceros, Form Z. He has complaints about all of these platforms. For example, he says, "Rhino is like 3D for dummies," adding, "Form Z produces gaps or leaks."[108] He sees CATIA as the system that finally gets things right. "It does everything you need," Laird says. And so he has confidence in CATIA, even without a deep technical understanding of how it works. "CATIA gives me the feeling that I have control when I use it. Other systems will only get to a certain point before crashing; not CATIA." Laird claims that he was hired at Paul Morris Associates because of his skill with computer-aided design. Often, he works exclusively on the computer or coordinates the computer-aided design work done by others, a role he and his peers call being the "keeper of the geometry." Clearly, Laird's professional identity is constructed around his relationship with computer-aided design. Although he has become Quix's best student with CATIA, he continues to see the software in his own way. For example, while Quix teaches CATIA as a means of establishing technical control over designs, in Laird's hands, CATIA also "feels artistic." For him, CATIA is a medium "for the manipulation of light and shadow."

A third phase of Quix's teaching is comprised of implementation with continuing resistance. In phrase three, designers at Paul Morris use CATIA, with Quix's oversight, for the design of a large project, a major public building. By this stage, the designers feel that using CATIA makes them part of the evolving direction of the firm. Yet, even at this point, resistance to CATIA continues, although it takes new forms. For example, despite his affection for CATIA, Laird has reservations about its practicality. He complains that it is not architects, but consultants and contractors who are its main beneficiaries: "It is focused on making someone else's job easier." Laird is concerned that at Paul Morris Associates people spend too much time modeling buildings on computers. "We are dumping hours into modeling." Laird's position is echoed by a senior designer who says that computer-aided design increases architects' tendency to "fetishize drawing" and create too many details too soon in the design process. Thus, even with CATIA's use mandated by the head of the firm, Quix is still on the defensive.

Indeed, within the firm, Rikle Shales has carved out her identity by avoiding CATIA altogether. In architecture school, Shales was something of a computer guru, the "go-to person" for other students. But in Paul Morris's office, Shales keeps her knowledge of modeling to herself. When she works on the computer, she sticks to two-dimensional programs; mostly, she communicates her ideas through sketches. Morris specifically asked her to learn CATIA, but although she voices some regret about this, Shales never got around to learning the program, something she explains as due to the weight of other responsibilities. She says, "I like to feel that I am keeping up with everything," but in fact, Shales's authority over the building project that "lives" on CATIA has been due, at least in part, to the fact that she has not learned the system. The time she has saved has freed her up to do project administration. Beyond this, not knowing CATIA has confirmed her with a non-technical identity; she is seen as a people person and a design person. Others describe her as the "glue" that holds projects together, organizes tasks within the firm, and coordinates communication with outside consultants.

While Quix and Laird forged their roles within the firm by identifying themselves with technology, Shales made her place by keeping it at arm's length. Paul Morris, the head of the firm, has done neither. He does not represent himself as a technical expert, but has allowed the technology to be an active player in his relationships with colleagues, most notably with a younger generation.

As this story continues in the next chapters, I will show how designers struggle to find a place for themselves in shared spaces emerging around new technologies for simulation. The story will expand beyond the boundaries of the architect's office to include the practices of acousticians, fire safety experts, structural engineers, mechanical engineers, and sustainability experts. For each of these identities, simulations are shaping new ways of being and challenging traditional divisions between creative and technical work. Architects still identify with art, and engineers still identify with science; but increasingly, each profession sees technology as a focus for discussions about how their values and their presence can be reasserted and even reconsidered.

Chapter 3

"Special Men" and Universal Machines

H. H. Richardson was a master architect. The nineteenth-century designer, best known for conceiving the Trinity Church in Boston, was an active participant in every aspect of his office's work. Today, in 2012, it is the computer that participates in every aspect of architecture, and practitioners are left asking: "Whither the role of the master?"

The work that Richardson formerly oversaw is now distributed in new and sometimes opaque ways among a network of specialists and computer simulations. At the 1963 Arup "Symposium on the Use of Computers in Architecture," one engineer predicted that "special men" would develop in architecture alongside computers. His suggestion that the profession would require new roles was far simpler than the reality today – that computers are shifting all roles. Increasingly, practitioners must define their relationships with computer simulations to position themselves in architecture. These new technologies are augmenting the reach of the master architect, and in parallel, the identity of each professional in the field.

New relationships are emerging among practitioners and their machines. People are more specialized and computers are increasingly ubiquitous. Each computer simulation is an instantiation of a "universal machine" or "universal Turing machine," a theoretical device conceived by artificial intelligence pioneer Alan Turing to carry out any algorithmic process.[109] Turing defined this ultimate machine as a conceptual set of elements: a tape (or linear memory); a device for reading and writing to the tape; a grammar or table of read, move, and write instructions; and a register for the current state of the machine. Today, these elements underlie the inner workings of every modern computer. Since Turing's ground-breaking work establishing the basis of modern digital computing, physical instantiations of his machine have evolved rapidly. What we call computers nowadays are miniature, but powerful, universal machines: their memories are expansive, their reading and writing capabilities function at high speeds, and their grammars deal with a vast range of operations. Theoretically, any activity that can be reduced to information processing can be reproduced by Turing's machine. Thus, Turing foresaw the computer as a pervasive device for simulation.

In the stories that follow, designers are negotiating complex relationships with and around simulations. They are finding that in order both to retain their disciplinary allegiances and adopt new practices of simulation, they must work between worlds. A master architect who cannot work directly on the screen keeps a hand in design through a special relationship with an apprentice who is an architect and also a hacker. An acoustician uses an immersive sound simulator to create a place where he can be both scientist and designer. A structural engineer gains credibility from his work with advanced simulations, but attributes his close relationships with architects to his ability to draw and to speak their language. A fire safety engineer has an understanding with regulators: she respects their rules, but uses simulations to bypass them when the rules limit her designs. Each of the individuals described in this chapter is a hybrid, discovering ways of being a designer that bridge old and new conceptions of practice in architecture.

The Architect

The master–apprentice relationship is being redefined in the context of technologies for geometric modeling. Theorists Donald Schön and Dana Cuff write about the strong tradition of the master–apprentice relationship.[110] Each argues, in their own way, that design is best understood through the relationship between the master and the apprentice. Dana Cuff writes that this is the "principal social relation" in architecture. Schön describes traditional design education through the intimate involvement of a master architect, Quist, in all the particulars of his student Petra's work. Schön illustrates how closely they work together, with Quist's hands on Petra's drawings:

> Quist places a sheet of tracing paper over Petra's sketches and begins to draw over her drawing. As he draws he talks. He says, for example, "the kindergarten might go here . . . then you might carry the gallery level through – and look down into here . . ."[111]

At Paul Morris Associates, geometric modeling software enables a reconfiguration of the master–apprentice relationship. Paul Morris is a prolific practitioner and retired academic who gained early acclaim for his striking modernist buildings. He belongs to a generation of which architectural theorist Reyner Banham writes, "Being unable to think without drawing had become the true mark of one fully socialized into the profession of architecture."[112] Morris still relies on a pencil to develop new ideas. However, within his office, computer modeling is replacing many of the traditional tasks of the pencil, such as drafting and rendering. And although Morris rarely touches the machine, it has transformed his personal practice as well. He often works on the concept phase of designs with an apprentice, usually a younger employee who can help him model a range of design ideas.

Drew Thorndike, one of the apprentices who works with Morris to prepare sketches for design competitions, has worked with geometric modeling since he was in college and continues to spend time learning new software. When asked about how design software figures in his long-term goals, Thorndike replies eagerly that they play "a big part . . . I want to stay ahead of the game . . . Computers equal speed, and if I don't learn the new software, I will be out of the market. I am convinced of that."[113]

From their first interactions on a project, a pattern emerges: Morris makes a sketch and Thorndike translates the sketch into a geometric model on the computer. Morris always asks Thorndike to print out the computer images he has generated. Then Morris and Thorndike sit together with a roll of tracing paper and, in a close variant on the practice of Quist and Petra that Schön writes about, Morris draws revisions over Thorndike's prints.

As the project progresses, Morris stops requesting prints and begins to look directly at the images on the computer. Now it is not unusual to hear Morris say to Thorndike, "Let's go look at your computer." The concept sketches are still drawn by Morris, but as projects progress, he and Thorndike work together at the computer; Thorndike operates the machine while Morris gives him guidance. From Thorndike's point of view, his boss has "learned to accept the technology on his own terms." From the point of view of others at the firm, Morris has conceded an important role, or as one puts it, "he is no longer the one sculpting space." But Morris has maintained what was most important to him: he wants to stay in touch with the evolving model, no matter where it is, even if he has to sacrifice some of the physical intimacy he has with pencil drawings.

As they work, Morris and Thorndike are looking at the same screen, but they are not seeing the same thing. For example, when Morris makes a sketch for a new public library, Thorndike's job at the computer is to translate it into the modeling program Rhinoceros, which he refers to as "Rhino." Thorndike usually sits at the computer while Morris stands behind him. Rhino presents them with the virtual equivalent of a blank sheet of paper, a faint Cartesian grid floating in boundless space. With a click of the mouse, Thorndike chooses a starting point for an arc defined by three points on its circumference. Next, he chooses a section of an ellipse. With these two design elements, Thorndike generates a curved surface for the library's facade. Thorndike is choosing from a predefined set of shapes that the computer knows. These are his "primitives." Morris is watching his design emerge; he does not see into

Rhino's inner world. Rhino produces each of its images by simulating thousands of rays of light that reflect off primitives in the model and penetrate a virtual "camera," a virtual eye. This technique, known as "ray tracing," is based on an early Renaissance mechanism for transferring three-dimensional objects onto a flat surface. So, for example, when Thorndike rotates the screen model, Rhino actually computes a new camera position for the ray-tracing algorithm. Thorndike understands how the image is being produced; Morris sees only the rotation and only the final image.

Morris is aware of the principles that drive Rhino's renderings, but when they talk about what is on the screen, Thorndike can make reference to details of Rhino's primitives and the ray-tracing algorithm. Morris can only talk about lines, surfaces, and colors, at best a snapshot of the design. Before the technology intervened, Morris worked with images on paper, which he could physically manipulate. Now his apprentice has a more direct experience of the developing design. Morris's experience is mediated, dependent. Maurice Merleau-Ponty suggests that people incorporate instruments into their physical sensibilities through the experience of manipulating them.[114] From this point of view, Morris and Thorndike each have a different experience and therefore a different understanding of the model. Morris's is more distant; Thorndike's is more embodied and internal.

As we can see, sharing a screen does not necessarily mean sharing a vision. It does bring, however, a new kind of intimacy that makes explicit what is shared and what is not. For even when software is celebrated and used creatively, certain former habits of mind endure. In particular, architects remain preoccupied with drawing, the expression of another kind of intimacy with volume and profile. Thorndike, the apprentice, believes that Paul Morris hired him not for his technical expertise, but for his ability to draw with a pencil. For Morris himself, who thinks with a pencil and is newly bound to an apprentice who can help him think on the screen, there are already intimations of a convergence. He has, after all, chosen a working partner who is both fluent on the screen and with a pencil. In an instrumental sense, it is Thorndike's ability with a computer program that makes him indispensable to Morris, but it is Thorndike's fluency with a pencil that probably makes Morris comfortable with him as a colleague.

Thorndike describes the evolving design for the library that he is modeling under the guidance of Morris: "The room is an elongated almond . . . The entrance is tight and tall and the center of the space is wide but the same height." As Thorndike speaks, he takes a thick dark pencil out of his pocket and draws the profile of the library onto the bare surface of one of the drafting tables. He is proud of his expertise with Rhino and other modeling software, but he, like his master, still thinks with a pencil; his identity as an architect, like Morris's, lies between technological worlds.

In such stories we see that the question, "Who am I in relation to software?" has become central to how architects negotiate professional identity. Paul Morris uses it as a tool to make buildings in partnership with computationally-savvy colleagues. But some architects are primarily masters of the virtual, securing international reputations in architectural competitions through objects that exist only on the screen. Their practices flourish on computers and in art galleries rather than on construction sites. Among them are architects who work with master programmers who are sometimes also architects. Such is the relationship between Craig Haig and Mike Orlov, both of whom work in an academic setting. Haig understands how the program operates, has a working model of its underlying operation, but cannot program the simulations that make his work possible. This role falls to Orlov, "his" master programmer. Haig is master of a realm he cannot completely enter. Orlov says of their partnership: "It's really funny, while we are communicating together about the same thing, we are talking about different levels of the same thing."

Here, as in other relationships among architects who approach geometric modeling with different levels of understanding, the technology acts as a trading zone. Architects work across their own cultural divides, whether it is Morris, the master, and Thorndike, the apprentice; or Haig, the virtual architect, and Orlov, his hacker partner. This terminology stresses the diversity in what different architects bring to negotiations with technology; another way to look at their exchanges is to stress similarities in what the software imposes on all of them. A program such as CATIA embodies culturally specific views of image-making. These will be transmitted to any user who engages with the program; that user will be drawn into the embrace not just of a specific program, but of a way of encoding reality.[115] Architectural theorist William Mitchell talks of software as "frozen ideology."[116] Anthropologist and engineer Gary Downey describes the power of computer-aided design as the subordination of design to computer graphics, a process in which one's eyes and fingers are given over to the machine.[117] In Michel Foucault's language, the program becomes a new kind of power, a force that "produces reality; it produces domains of objects and rituals of truth."[118]

The passage above describes the changing professional dynamics between masters and apprentices. But it is illustrative of broader shifts in the social organization of architectural work. New technologies for simulating buildings are not simply a means to an end. They mediate relationships, reconfiguring the social and conceptual spaces in which designers compete for control. However, the negotiations between architects must be seen as part of a broader system of professionals. In what follows, I turn to the identities of specialists in architecture, mostly engineers, through stories of individuals working at Arup. Once considered merely consultants, these technical experts are increasingly at the center of debates over what architecture can accomplish. They are part of a movement toward increasing technical sophistication in design.

Throughout her work, Sherry Turkle considers how technologies create new intimacies in everyday life. She explains that people adopt technologies, not necessarily for what technologies do for them in a pragmatic sense, but for how technologies make them feel. When we call technologies "tools," we underestimate their evocative power. They do not simply allow us to act on the world, they act on us; as extensions of our bodies and our minds, technologies transform our sense of self. "We make our technologies, and they, in turn, shape us," writes Turkle.[119] This is as true in professional arenas as it is in the personal settings that are the focus of her work. Practitioners in architecture use simulations not only to evaluate their buildings in the world, but also to position themselves in the field. Using Arup as a lens on the practices of highly technical individuals in architecture, I examine new roles and relationships in three arenas: acoustics, structures, and fire safety. In each of these domains, specialists have made footholds by bridging worlds. Like

Figure 6
The Arup SoundLab.

Thorndike, they must do two things to define their professional positions. They must differentiate themselves, but they must also establish meaningful connections. In the work of all designers, the use of computer simulation must be both technically justifiable and culturally palatable.

The Acoustician

"The problem with old school acoustics using the Sabine formula is that you were doing acoustics in a very one dimensional way," explains Francis Martin, a member of the Arup Acoustics Group. According to Martin, the Sabine formula, a numerical means of simulating architectural acoustics, constrains professional relationships. Martin elaborates, "[Y]ou were having to do the calculations and then say to the architect, this is what's wrong with your room." He associates Sabine's formula, a simple equation derived early in the twentieth century to predict the reverberation time of sound in a room – the time it takes for an emitted sound to decay to inaudibility – with "old school" acoustics and outmoded professional roles. The formula can be expressed in the following form:[120]

$$t = \frac{.164\,V}{\Sigma\,(a_n\,s_n)}$$

in which:

t = reverberation time (s)

V = volume of room (m^3)

a_n = absorption coefficient of material n

s_n = surface area of material n (m^2).

This equation sets up a constricted space of alternatives shared among acousticians and their collaborators, shaped exclusively around the measurement and evaluation of a single value. In response, Martin and his team have developed an alternative, immersive simulation, which they call the Arup SoundLab, to expand the shared space of alternatives in acoustics and, correspondingly, their relationships with a broad range of design participants.

The Arup SoundLab is both a literal space, in which collaborators can "listen to a building" together before it is built, and a conceptual space, in which participants can form a consensus about how good architecture should present itself to the ear.[121] Martin explains that working with architects in the Arup SoundLab has led to improved collaborations:

> We can relate to architects much better. If we are brought on board at the ideal time, which is if we are brought on board at concept, we can sit with the architect and we can say . . . this is what you have to work with. They can hear and they can understand it. Then from

> their first ideas and concepts they are much more willing to work with us when we talk to them about shape and form.[122]

Martin works to bring clients and collaborators into the Arup SoundLab during the early phases of design in order to educate them in the physics and poetics of sound. In the process, Martin defines his role as the orchestrator of discussions about form from an acoustical perspective. Architectural form has traditionally been the core responsibility of architects. However, Martin is not an architect, nor is he purely a scientist. He is between these professional worlds and his professional identity in architecture depends on his ability to bridge the gap. Martin's accounts about collaboration in the Arup SoundLab present design practice as a system of relationships in flux, in which participants are in a continual struggle to define their position. For Martin and his colleagues, creating a place within this system means negotiating relationships with other people, but also with technology. Martin is one of a number of technical specialists in architecture today, all of whom must find ways of positioning themselves through varying levels of engagement with simulations.

Wallace Sabine was a professor of physics at Harvard University in 1900, when he derived the formula for reverberation time. Although he had been working on the physics of sound for years and based his work on a long history of discoveries by other physicists, he condensed his findings into a simple equation (see above) in the context of two architectural consulting projects: a lecture hall at Harvard's Fogg Museum and the Boston Symphony Hall, considered by Martin to be "one of the three best performance halls in the world." Sabine did not initiate the science of acoustics, but he established a space for acousticians in architecture. One of the first scientists working in the realm of building design, he became a model of the modern architectural acoustician, a new professional identity.

In *The Soundscape of Modernity*, historian Emily Thompson explains that Sabine was given a prominent position in the design of the Boston Symphony Hall by philanthropist Henry Lee Higginson, owner of the Boston Symphony Orchestra.[123] Initially, Higginson and his architects, McKim, Mead, and White, considered existing techniques of acoustical design. Higginson turned to Sabine to ensure an aural triumph. Sabine enjoyed a productive collaboration with McKim, Mead, and White. However, his presence displaced the traditional role of the architect as acoustical expert.

Since at least the eighteenth century, architects have been using drawings to analyze the propagation of sound in buildings. Such geometric methods can be applied on the same paper where plans are laid out, allowing abstract architectural form to be the instrument of acoustical control. More often than not, however, in the design of performance halls, architects have reproduced the tested geometry of traditional auditoriums. This approach is

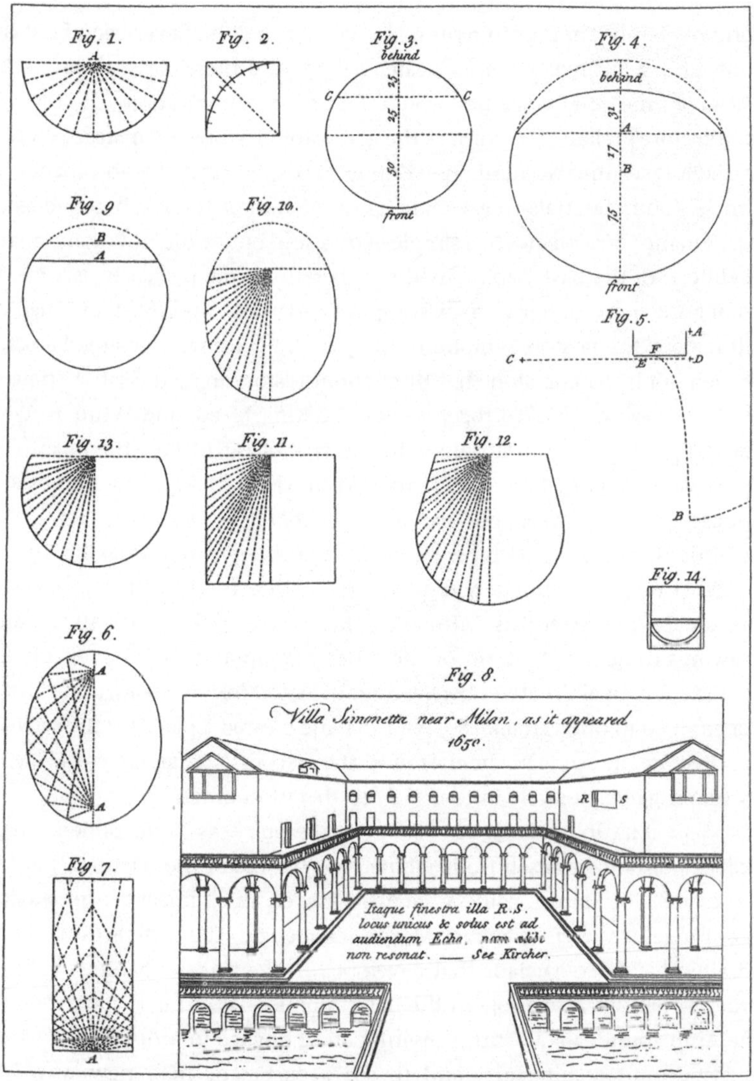

Figure 7
Illustrations by George Saunders demonstrate a geometric approach to architectural acoustics.

meant to replicate the acoustics of great spaces of the past, but despite architects' adherence to tradition, there is little certainty in it. New concert halls rarely mirror the conditions in time-tested designs, for they must also accommodate the features of different sites, climates, performance groups, and, inevitably, larger crowds.

Somewhat unconventionally, McKim, Mead, and White first proposed a Greek theater plan for the Boston Symphony Hall. However, there were no good precedents with which to confirm the acoustic merit of such a form. As Emily Thompson writes, "No concert hall had ever been built in the form of a semicircular amphitheater before, and there was no way to know ahead of time how such a hall would sound."[124] Sabine's approach veered from architecture's reliance on form as the generator of acoustics. Instead, the Sabine formula takes into account the volume of a space and the absorbency of its construction materials to calculate its reverberation time. Sabine reduced the performance of acoustics to a simple expression, but he did not totally abandon traditions of the past. Sabine used reverberation time primarily as a means of comparing new designs to existing concert halls approved by Higginson. Ultimately, the Boston Symphony Hall was built using a rectangular scheme, proven not by Sabine alone but throughout history to be the safest choice.

Sabine worked together with McKim, Mead, and White to develop the design, but he was left alone in the task of calculating the reverberation time. Sabine retained a scientific role. Meanwhile, McKim saw him as a great counsellor and advisor, but not as a collaborating designer. Sabine moved acoustics into a quantitative zone, apart from the realm of drawing, the realm of the visual, and ultimately the realm of architects. His work made acoustics opaque to non-scientists. Although there were still conversations around drawings to define the form of the Boston Symphony Hall's auditorium, the shared space of alternatives between Sabine and McKim, Mead, and White was constrained to one variable. So, while Sabine created a place for the scientist in architecture, in doing so, he narrowed the discourse on architectural acoustics by framing it exclusively in terms of reverberation time.

Martin characterizes Sabine's discourse as "one dimensional" in order to distance himself from Sabine and the role of the scientist that Sabine represents. For Martin, being a scientist or even an engineer means staying on the fringes of form-making. Martin challenges the interactions between architects and acousticians that developed in the wake of Sabine's formula in order to take an active role in the determination of form. Through the use of the Arup SoundLab, Martin is inviting all to engage in a new discourse about acoustics and architecture, and to see acousticians in a new way. Martin introduced me to the use of the term co-designer in this setting. He explains the co-designer in this way: "We become a collaborator. Not the engineer. We don't usurp the role of the designer, but we become a collaborator in the design process."

Martin's distinction between the approach to acoustics characterized by the Sabine formula and his own approach, using the Arup SoundLab, recalls the sociologist Max Weber's distinction between the ethics of the scientist and those of the politician.[125] Weber explains the vocation of science as the pursuit of clarity. Scientists follow an "ethic of ultimate ends," in which the ends justify the means. "The believer in an ethic of ultimate ends feels responsible only for seeing to it that the flame of pure intentions is not squelched."[126]

Weber contrasts this with the politician's "ethic of responsibility." For Weber, being a politician means giving priority to the legitimacy of the means over the ends. In their shift from the optimization of reverberation time to the pursuit of a consensus in the Arup SoundLab, acousticians have traded the ethics of the scientist for those of the politician. By focusing on a collaborative means of examining architectural acoustics, Martin and his colleagues have created a place for themselves as engaged co-designers rather than objective scientists.

The acousticians at Arup challenge Sabine's approach to acoustics through their use of the Arup SoundLab. They reintroduce form as a variable in acoustics, whereas Sabine only considered volume and material absorbency. They render reverberation time aurally, rather than numerically, bringing it into the realm of common experience. They seek to expand the space of alternatives set up by Sabine's formula. Instead of searching for an optimal reverberation time, they build a consensus among design participants. Their work has opened a new space in which the performance of architectural acoustics can be evaluated by technical and non-technical participants together, a virtual space of shared experience.

With their new technology, acousticians at Arup are working toward a language of objectified, replicable, and controllable acoustic experience. Once a common vocabulary is developed, participants can identify distinct sound events and compare their salient characteristics. The ability to perform this kind of shared comparison is the "killer app" of the Arup SoundLab. The result is a more controlled conversation.

This is part of a strategic professional agenda for Arup acousticians. They are able not only to engage in closer collaborations with architects, but also to claim a new competitive niche within architecture by presenting the human experience of buildings as accessible through science and technology, and thus a point of access for scientific and technical consultants.

Through new ways of knowing harnessed in simulations like the Arup SoundLab, technical practitioners challenge older architectural conceptions of experience. In a previous era, phenomenologist architect Norberg-Schulz explained experience as indivisible, holistic, and unpredictable.[127] Martin and his colleagues assert quite the opposite: that experience can be compartmentalized and predicted in areas like acoustics using computer simulations as instruments of control. Experience in buildings has been reduced to another professional problem through which designers can claim jurisdiction. Acousticians at Arup have gained some leverage by balancing dual identities as scientists and co-designers.

Like all professionals, acousticians are prone to defining themselves in terms of their interactions with others. At Arup, acousticians see a competitive advantage in presenting their roles as accommodating and collaborative, rather than autonomous. They alternatively call themselves consultants, collaborators, co-designers, and only occasionally designers. Linus Russell, an acoustician at Arup, describes himself as a "room designer" because of the "holistic way" in which he looks at acoustical spaces. Others, like Martin, are wary of usurping the title of designer. The uncertainty of their identities is particularly evident in Arup's involvement in architectural competitions, in collaboration with architects and other designers. In many selective contests, Arup's people are able to participate on more than one team. This is because, despite their intimate role in design, Arup employees are often not considered part of the design team. What emerges from these occasions is the sense that professional relationships at Arup are dynamic. Martin explains it this way:

> It's depending on the project. On some days I am the acoustician in a long line of other consultants and on some projects I'm the client's direct friend and advisor, the person they look to for the right advice for dealing with the issues, and it varies from project to project, purely based on relationship and the time you've known the people or whatever.[128]

Martin's story illustrates the unsettled nature of relationships in design practice. Sometimes, when Martin can find shared ground with clients, he takes on the role of a collaborator. At other times, he is simply a consultant. Simulations like the Arup SoundLab reveal a contingent, highly specific image of architecture, in which it is difficult to separate technical expertise from design work.

In Chapter 1, I characterized a broad range of practitioners in architecture as designers. Clearly, the use of the term "designer" in practice is not so simple. Martin's identification with the role of co-designer is illustrative of the subtlety with which professionals define their place. Indeed, any claim to a professional identity in architecture must contend with the claims of countless other professionals competing for jurisdiction. Such claims must situate one strategically within this system, and they must be defensible. Although I will continue to use the term "designers" to characterize a range of professionals, my intention is not to oversimplify their accounts. On the contrary, I am making a point that all participants hold positions of authorship to varying degrees. In this sense, I mean the term "designers" to be representative of the complex, uncertain, and rapidly changing set of creative roles in architecture. All participants are designers and all designers are co-designers.

The Structural Engineer

Acousticians like Martin position themselves professionally by using simulations to bring architects and others into an experience of acoustics. Other technical specialists have discovered their own methods of professional positioning. Aldus Barnes, a structural engineer by training and member of the Advanced Geometry Unit (AGU) at Arup, has formed many successful collaborations and earned a prominent place for himself in architecture by adopting the language and skills of architects. "Talk in terms of texture and density, instead of torsion and shear. That way they don't think you are just another nerd," Barnes advises the young members of his team. He has gained media attention for his collaborations with high-profile architects like James Stirling, Rem Koolhaas, and Toyo Ito. A recent newspaper article explains that Barnes's primary talents lie in his skill as a collaborator, noting that "beyond making their projects buildable, his solutions open such architects to explore forms they might not have considered before."[129] For Barnes, advanced computer simulations are merely a means of proving his concepts. "The computer is an enabler, but it is never the conceptual model," says Barnes. He explains the prominence of sketching and the limited role of computing in his work. "Sketches are the means of developing the conceptual model or diagram. The thinking model is made into a spatial model in the computer. The computer reveals the finer[-]grain logic."

Barnes gains credibility from the computer simulations that the Advanced Geometry Unit creates for a range of audiences. However, his intimate collaborations with architects and artists are based on his ability to speak the language of architecture and, perhaps just as importantly, his ability

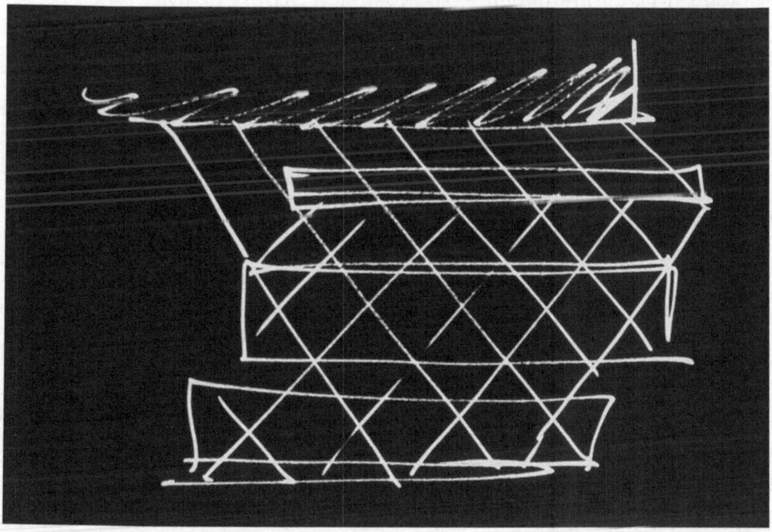

Figure 8
A sketch of the Seattle Public Library by Aldus Barnes, a project he worked on with Rem Koolhaas.

Figure 9
The Seattle Public Library.

to draw. Barnes's closest partners, like Koolhaas, have told him that he has a special skill in devising abstract models through drawings. Barnes calls his drawings "thinking models" and "concept diagrams." These representations get a project going and provide it with a point of reference throughout development. For Barnes, drawings capture the essence of a building concept.

"When I discovered my talent for abstraction," says Barnes, "I thought it was a unique gift." Soon enough, Barnes realized he was "better at abstracting ideas than many architects." Later, he learned that this was something that all engineers are taught to do; it was not his gift alone. However, he has learned to combine his ability to capture design concepts with drawing, out of an interest in working with architects on form-making, and exploring how issues of structure meet issues of aesthetics. Barnes argues that these interests have put him in a unique position at Arup; he sees himself as a designer among technicians.

Barnes the structural engineer and Martin the acoustician describe their relationships with architects in very different ways. For Martin, advanced simulations are at the center of these relationships; the Arup SoundLab bridges the technical means of acousticians and the needs of architects. Barnes prefers working on architects' terms. His use of advanced simulations is often merely supportive. For example, in his collaboration with the architect Rem Koolhaas on the China Central Television (CCTV) building in Beijing, advanced simulations were used in what he calls a "technocratic way." The project required "a ferocious amount of computation," says Barnes. Koolhaas had to wait six months while Barnes and his engineers did the calculations on their own. It was an example of the use of simulation as "muscle."[130] However, when it comes to intervening in the design process and not just evaluating solutions, Barnes finds drawing to be most useful.

Among both engineers and architects, making drawings with a pencil is described as working by hand. The pencil is a transparent part of design; the computer is not, and it can bring unwanted associations and constraints. Barnes is not alone in his preference for drawing as a form of presence and a language of exchange with architects. Halden Harrison, also a structural engineer, says that sketching is an important part of developing a good rapport with architects. Drawing, for Harrison, is a means to understand "what [architects] want to achieve" and "[how] to interpret it." Drawing can be seen as a kind of simple simulation. It allows engineers like Barnes and Harrison to reconstruct architects' designs using a familiar medium, even if it is only the pencil in their hands. The notion that drawing is a form of simulation is subtly suggested in Barnes's characterization of his drawings as "abstract models." Barnes's drawings interpret the design intent that architects bring to their collaborations and make room for structural concerns. Often his work blurs the boundaries between the concerns of engineering and the concerns of architecture. In 2002, Barnes collaborated with Toyo Ito on the Serpentine Pavilion in Hyde Park, London. Barnes made extensive use of his engineering knowledge of structures and computation to work on the project, but his goals were aesthetic, architectural:

> I thought about the rhythm of the lines intersecting. It was a rectangular container but we wanted to undermine its containment factor. I thought that the intersection of lines would create such a puzzle for your eye that your eye would travel through the cell. It's an aesthetic game. That gives pleasure to the eye.[131]

Such accounts are illustrative of Barnes's desire to move beyond the traditional division between architects and engineers. However, he has met resistance from architects. The newspaper article on Barnes reproaches him for trying to push past his own professional boundaries, suggesting that he "has decided that the title of engineer is not enough."[132] Barnes's stance is that he focuses on building, rather than on lines of professional jurisdiction; however, he is finding that these lines are well guarded.

Barnes gains technical leverage in the world of architects by using advanced simulations, but he challenges the perceived distinction between architects and engineers through his ability to engage in projects with a combination of an architect's skill with drawing and an engineer's mind for abstract thinking. Barnes has gained notoriety, positive and negative, by moving between worlds. Here, as in the case of Martin, professional labels do not adhere.

There are other examples of technical specialists at Arup who leverage their ability to draw in collaborations with architects. Richard Wells is a British mechanical engineer who relies almost exclusively on sketches and hand calculations. He works for the Arup Facade Group and his expertise is in understanding material properties and assemblies. Wells is satisfied using a pencil to work out technical facade details. "I haven't used CAD in thirteen to fourteen years," he says proudly.[133]

Wells shows me a typical project report for a terminal building at Heathrow Airport in the UK, in which most of the drawings are done with a pencil, and explains, "we are working in a niche where we do a lot of hand sketches." He says that sketches allow you to share ideas quickly and to integrate different perspectives. In Wells's view, sketching leads to more inclusive spaces of alternatives. He explains sketches as "faster" and "more democratic," adding, "when we meet with the architects, we can do these sketches together, live." For Wells, sketching not only involves the team, it also acknowledges the openness of teamwork. In other words, "it reflects the fact that this is not a finished design. People know we are still exploring options." Wells asserts that sketching is inclusive, open, and also inherently thoughtful. When he sees his collaborators working "by hand," he notices that "they don't turn off their critical faculties the way they do with some computer drawings." For Barnes, being able to draw puts him in a position of power. Wielding a pencil enables him to control the design in its most essential form. Wells sees drawing as an ethical choice. Keeping his hand present in design is Wells's means of encouraging a democratic and reflective shared space of alternatives.

Although Wells is able to develop a rapport with architects by adopting the traditional architectural medium of drawing, he attributes the overall success of facade design at Arup to the technical prowess of its engineers and the comparative "deskilling of architects." From Wells's perspective, there are new functional demands on facades, and architects have reacted by moving away from expertise in materials and the technical aspects of building. Some of these demands have come from legislation, explains Wells; standards are being pushed up for energy efficiency. But architects are also just envisioning more complex facades without an understanding of how to design them. Wells says that this trend is part of a new movement that has brought an increased interest in complex shapes. He explains that architects expect new kinds of facades, especially glass facades, to serve a wide variety of purposes: expressive, structural, and environmental.

According to Wells, contemporary facade designs have necessitated a new, rigorous, technical approach. But he does not equate this approach with computers, and resists the notion that Arup's success in the area of facade design was enabled by computer simulations. Although Wells acknowledges that some facade designers are using "heavy modeling" to analyze and enable facades that are particularly elaborate, for day-to-day design, simple rules and experiments with full-size mockups suffice.[134] "I don't use my computer for much more than e-mail," he proclaims.

Wells, Harrison, and Barnes acknowledge the usefulness of computer simulations, but are wary of their potential to get in the way of collaboration. These designers have created roles for themselves in architecture by translating their technical knowledge into drawing, a language of exchange they share with architects. Even as some architects are becoming more technologically competent, Wells, Harrison, and Barnes do not see computer simulations as spaces in which to meet architects eye to eye. Rather, they try to meet architects on their home turf. They turn to computer simulations only to highlight the areas where architect-designed schemes are technically weak.

Andrew Werner agrees with his colleagues at Arup that "the new technology of building facades is not something that an architect can master."[135] Werner works from a belief that "there used to be a master builder, but that no longer is the case." However, unlike Wells, Harrison, and Barnes, he focuses almost exclusively on the use of computer simulations to leverage his technical know-how. He works on facade design, but not in the same group as Wells. Werner started work with the Arup Facade Group in 2000, but now works with Arup's Environmental Physics Group. He is trained as both a civil and a structural engineer with a PhD in building physics, which is not typical in practice for engineers or architects. In addition to his pragmatic goals for each project, Werner maintains broader academic interests. He wants to understand how current simulation tools can be used more effectively; he wants to "understand their limits." Werner and Wells are both working on facade design, but in very different contexts.

The Environmental Physics Group does about 80 percent of its work for others within Arup, as a means of enhancing the services provided by a typical building team. Only 20 percent of the group's time is spent with external clients like architects. Thus, Werner acts primarily as an internal consultant. He does not stress the importance of drawing. Instead, he uses technical languages to collaborate with other specialists at Arup. This differentiates Werner's work from that of Wells. Wells feels that he must define his professional position through a collaborative process of drawing with architects. In contrast, on the rare occasions when Werner does work with architects, he describes it as "taking them on a tour" of technical issues, with computer simulations as his maps. Werner does not share the intimate collaborations that some of his colleagues have with architects.

Wells, Harrison, Barnes, and Martin are part of a tradition of collaboration at Arup. In the early days of the firm, Ove Arup built a reputation on his relationships with architects like Berthold Lubetkin and Jørn Utzon. In Wells's ongoing work, we can see a continuation of the traditional architect–engineer relationship, but we can also see new boundaries drawn in areas like facade design, where engineers are now the experts. Although facade design has been the domain of architects at least as far back as the Renaissance, Wells brings an approach which is specialized and highly technical, if not computational. Wells's methods of practice are engineering methods. He does not take up Barnes's interest in the aesthetic qualities of buildings, the qualities that architects are most likely to address. Meanwhile, Werner works more closely with simulations, but within a more constrained context. He does not often work with architects, and when he does, it is not an open exchange. Structural engineers need to collaborate with architects, but there are many ways of establishing what will be traded and how.

The Fire Safety Engineer

"If you get the science right, then you can get the engineering right." This was the perspective of Dave Rasbash and Philip Thomas, two prominent engineers and fire researchers who ran a government center called the Fire Research Station in Borehamwood, England in the 1950s.[136] In that moment during the early development of modern fire regulations in England, material rules of building safety were scientifically codified and broadly implemented. Rasbash and Thomas were working with the conception that prescriptive rules can make buildings safe. This was the epistemological context in which Amelia Pearce of the Arup Fire Group began her career.[137]

Pearce's early work at the Fire Research Station provides a counterpoint to the simulation-based practice that she established years later at Arup. She began work at the Fire Research Station after graduating with an education in physics and mathematics. The Fire Research Station taught her that basic research was the basis for fire safety knowledge. She conducted fire-resistance experiments and tests on elements of structure that were then translated into rules, axioms, and facts – the foundations for prescriptive building regulations all over England. In contrast, Pearce's later work at Arup was contingent and project-specific. In practice, Pearce found that knowledge could not easily be reduced to a material measure of architecture. Knowledge in practice, particularly when seen through the lenses of simulations, only adhered to the particularities of a project: its context, clients, and transient occupancy conditions. When she eventually embraced practice, and simulations as her tool set, Pearce traded the epistemology of prescription for an epistemology of performance. In the process, she found a new stance from which to answer fire safety questions and a new role for herself in architecture.

Amelia Pearce's experience illustrates a broad shift in the locus of knowledge in architecture, from institutions like the Fire Research Station, a centralized space of knowledge production and dissemination, to project teams – loose, distributed networks of architects, engineers, clients, software developers, and institutional researchers. This change was enabled by new technologies for simulating some of the effects of fire. Pearce and others followed the shift to computer simulation and found prominent positions in practice, as highly connected nodes within the new networks of design knowledge. However, the transition from centrally located, prescriptive knowledge to distributed, performance-based knowledge had a material and historical context. It evolved slowly as a series of professional opportunities for designers, only visible through a combination of new architectural questions and new capabilities inherent in computer simulations.

In post-World War II London, innovative materials and building types prompted a new set of questions from regulators. Lightweight curtain-wall cladding with no fire resistance started to be used widely in the UK. Building regulators were worried about the ability of these new facades to keep heat from radiating across streets and spaces between buildings in the event of a fire. At the time, regulations did not prescribe the size of windows and no one had a good idea about how fire behaved in enclosed spaces, or how it might radiate out from lightweight curtain-wall facades. One of the important questions became: what is a reasonable distance between two buildings, if one has a lightweight curtain wall?

At the Fire Research Station, Pearce was set to the task of addressing the curtain wall safety problem. She began to collect information on what kinds of fires could be expected in buildings. A domestic building, for example, was not likely to have much combustible material; the ratio of such material to floor area would be quite low. These assumptions were built into the existing regulations. Pearce looked at these ratios to determine the maximum intensity of fires in typical spaces. At the same time, there was a lot of work being done on radiation and fire spreading because of the impending threat of nuclear war. Thus, Pearce had information on both architectural types and the ignition of materials by radiation. Using this available but generic information, Pearce was able to produce two tables which became the basis for new regulations on lightweight curtain wall facades. Unfortunately, legal restrictions prevented the regulations from specifying the distance between buildings; they could only specify the distance from the property line. So the regulation was set at half the minimum distance that Pearce found appropriate. This is how prescriptive regulations were developed at the Fire Research Station. Their work produced universal rules, based on a lot of assumptions about both construction practices and buildings in use.

The gap between generic rules and specific architecture problems meant that in addition to developing regulations, Pearce and her colleagues at the Fire Research Station had to answer numerous "What if?" questions from practitioners. During these years, Pearce was not only a researcher; she was already becoming an informal consultant to designers. The members of the Fire Research Station tried to look at fire safety from first principles and develop models to describe how buildings would behave in fires. "What if?" questions could be answered by reference to these underlying fire safety models; however, the practice was exhausting. Pearce happened to be quite good at it, though. She liked solving real problems. Her favorite part was figuring out the best way to deliver the answer – a complex process of translation. The universal rules developed by the Fire Research Station had to be adjusted for the specific conditions of the design and for the understanding of the client. For instance, architects always wanted to see the solution presented visually. Eventually, handling all the "What if?" questions became overwhelming. Solving for various scenarios became one of Pearce's main tasks. She started publishing on how to design for fire safety in an effort to extend universal rules and make them more approachable by designers, but her publications could not answer every contingency. The problem with the tests done at the Fire Research Station and the regulations that are based on those tests is that they assume simplistic conditions. Meanwhile, as Pearce explains, "in a fire, everything is transient." Experience in buildings occurs in specific conditions. Knowledge of experience will inherently be partial and contingent. Talcott Saunders, a veteran fire safety engineer who has worked with Pearce, explains that "technically, a fire is a fire, but there are differences."[138] For instance, the flow of people is different in London and in Hong Kong. In Hong Kong, says Saunders, people are not as concerned with personal space, so more of them might pass through a doorway at the same time. This leads to different patterns of movement and different needs for emergency evacuation. Knowledge about fire safety is local knowledge.

Practitioners in fire safety often educate clients, collaborators, and regulators in the prescriptive knowledge of local building regulations around the world and help them conform to these standards. As we have seen, these practitioners also help to establish such regulations. However, in the face of an increasingly diversified field of architecture, the limitations of prescriptive knowledge have become apparent. Today, in 2012, practitioners are proposing alternative ways of knowing through computer simulations to alleviate the concerns of building regulators in cases where the prescriptive knowledge of local building regulations poses unacceptable limitations on design.

Only after accepting a position at Arup did Amelia Pearce begin to see computer simulations at work in other disciplines, including structural and mechanical engineering. In these new technologies, she saw opportunities to address the issues of uncertainty that had plagued her at the Fire Research Station. Two projects in particular, Stansted Airport in the UK and the Lloyd's of London building, were significant in Pearce's adoption of simulations and her subsequent transformation into a practitioner.

During the 1980s, building regulators in London began to express concern about fire safety in large enclosed public spaces. Vast indoor atriums were becoming prevalent in an increasing number of building types, including shopping centers, airport terminals, and office atriums.[139] However, existing regulations constrained the floor area in these spaces. "In general, the codes set a limit of 45m travel distance to the nearest exit. When the floor layout is not known they set a limit of 30m distance drawn on plan to the nearest exit," wrote Pearce in a paper about fire safety in terminal buildings.[140] Large, closed public spaces represented a new typology for building regulators in London, who could not judge how smoke, fire, and people might move and interact in such circumstances. The Lloyd's of London building, an office tower in central London, designed by the architecture office of Richard Rogers Partnership, proposed an unusual multi-storey atrium, open at each floor. Pearce was hired to act as a consultant to Rogers. The Lloyd's building was among the first projects in which Pearce and her team struggled with regulators over the issue of fire safety in this new typology and what it meant for the limits of knowledge in architecture.

For the Lloyd's building, Pearce was able to obtain a relaxation from London regulators by proposing smoke-flow simulations as a means of jointly examining the safety of the atrium space. A physicist working with Pearce adopted computational fluid dynamics (CFD), a method of discretization used to approximate the behavior of flows. At Arup, this method had been used to conduct airflow analysis by mechanical engineers. Pearce and her assistant appropriated the method to calculate smoke flows in the Lloyd's atrium. But the CFD calculations produced little more than numbers. "One of the problems is actually illustrating the results of the calculations," says Pearce. For building regulators concerned about the Lloyd's atrium, Pearce presented the results of calculations as two-dimensional flows in a sectional drawing of the building. She used this drawing as a crude simulation, a virtual stand-in for the real building. Arup's practitioners, Rogers' architects, and London's regulators could see how the building would be safe before it was completed in 1986. Like Martin the acoustician, Pearce created a space of shared virtual experience, and positioned herself as its guide.

In their work on another project, Stansted Airport, a vast terminal completed in 1991 outside London, Pearce and her colleagues revised their use of computer simulations to once again bypass building regulations. Stansted was conceived by architects at Foster and Partners to maximize flexibility. Inside the terminal, the architects proposed small shops, like stalls, open to the larger space. Pearce explains that "existing terminals were often a series of small rooms. Stansted, on the other hand, was to be one vast room."[141] According to Pearce, the idea was to encourage passengers to drift in and out of the shops. However, the lack of compartmentalization worried regulators. The building

Figure 10 Lloyd's of London building: interior atrium.

regulations still called for an exit every 30 meters. Standing in the middle of Stansted's terminal space, a passenger would be 50 meters from the nearest exit. Pearce argues that in such circumstances, the regulations display limited foresight:

> When the code was written, they hadn't thought of this type of building. You tend to legislate on what you know about. You can't legislate something you [don't] know. Nobody ever thought you were going to put a great big roof over a whole high street of shops.[142]

Figure 11 Stansted Airport terminal interior.

To educate the regulators, members of Pearce's fire group constructed a visual demonstrating how people and smoke might behave within the controversial open floor plan at Stansted. "This involved our collecting a range of data from experiments, surveys, and fire statistics to illustrate how various measures could compensate for a lack of compartmentation," explains Pearce. Her physicist assistant did the computational fluid dynamics calculations once again. The calculations showed that smoke would take 12 minutes to descend to head height in several different circumstances. Pearce's team combined the calculations with empirical data from observations of passenger activity at existing terminals. They measured "walking speeds of people in the baggage reclaim area, which we thought was reasonably conservative because they would be carrying their baggage." Pearce then turned to the emerging field of computer graphics to represent the team's conclusions. With enthusiasm, she explains her discovery of a new medium of communication:

> I had seen computer graphics of structures, which looked like photographs of structures. They were drawings, but computer generated. They looked absolutely fantastic so I got in touch with them and said, "[L]ook we are trying to show what it would look like if you were here and had to get out of the building."[143]

As in the case of the Lloyd's building diagram, the Stansted graphics represented a shared space for Arup, Foster and Partners, and building regulators. Although the visuals seem crude by today's standards, they conform to what we expect of a contemporary simulation: on-screen, color images of the building, no mere diagram. They represented a great achievement in projecting human experience in buildings. Regulators readily accepted the new medium as a proxy for the real experience of the building, reassured that passengers could escape from the terminal although it spanned a distance much greater than their regulations typically allowed.

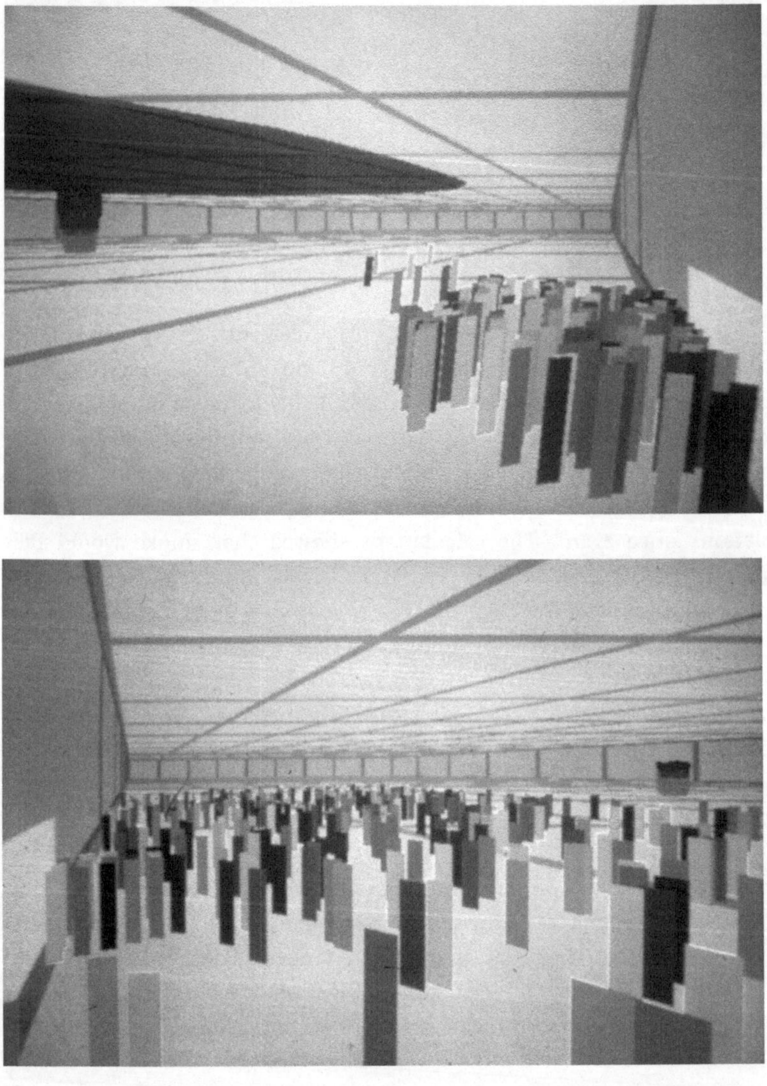

Figure 12
Frames from a smoke simulation of Stansted Airport.

Figure 12 The final simulated frame shows the slowest imagined occupant, an elderly person with a cane.

The story of the Fire Group at Arup illustrates how new identities can arise around technologies for simulation. The tools and techniques that allowed Amelia Pearce and her colleagues to bring together experimental, observational, and mathematical evidence to create believable experiential predictions about buildings also brought together professionals in new ways. Architects, engineers, and regulators could share and reflect upon the virtual experience of a building in distress. As with the Arup SoundLab, Pearce's fire simulations created an expanded space of shared alternatives. In Pearce's capable hands, computer simulations became powerful communication devices. Pearce bridged the needs of architects and regulators. In the process, she created a new center for herself and her colleagues, where the "What if?" questions of architecture can be asked and answered collectively.

A System of Identities

Professionals in architecture define their roles within a system of relationships. Increasingly, computer simulations frame these relationships and become the objects of intensely felt connections themselves. In this chapter, I have examined how architectural identities are negotiated within new cultures of simulation. The master architect, Morris, the acoustician, Martin, the structural engineer, Barnes, and the fire safety engineer, Pearce, must find new ways of being at the center of the architectural questions and discussions that are important to them.

The center is no longer the point of oversight held by nineteenth-century architect, H. H. Richardson. That position, the place of the master architect, has shifted. But this shift has made room for new configurations of people and machines. Morris, the master who once occupied the center of his architecture practice, now shares that space with others like Thorndike and the software, Rhino, which he harnesses. Meanwhile, we see new centers developing in relationship to specialized questions in acoustics, structures, and fire safety. Martin, Barnes, and Pearce have each found ways of being at the center, but not without new connections to both people and machines. They have used computer simulations to reorganize the division of labor around themselves. Martin has created a new focused space for discussions of acoustics. Barnes has become a translator of architectural ideas into abstract models necessary for computation. Pearce has destabilized the authority of regulations and in the process, positioned computer simulations as the place where all knowledge about fire safety can come together. In order to define new centers within the system of architecture, these practitioners have become hybrids, neither just designers, nor just technicians; they have learned to bridge worlds.

Hybrid professionals must do two things to gain credibility. They must differentiate themselves and they must establish a shared space of alternatives with other participants in design. In the cases examined in this chapter, I have found that simulations play significant but varied roles in this process of professional positioning. When simulations are brought to the center by practitioners, they can bridge the means of science and engineering and the needs of clients. Sometimes this just means that engineers are taking architects "on a tour" of technical issues, using simulations. However, some professionals at Arup see computer simulations as new spaces of equalization in which design decisions can be made through consensus. Yet for others, new simulations cannot replace sketching as a democratic space of design. However, in areas of design that focus on the experience of buildings, like acoustics and fire safety, computer simulations enable a discussion that is not possible through sketches. Here advanced simulations create a shared virtual space of collaboration in which various participants can develop a common language.

These stories illustrate the diversity and dynamism of professional identities in architecture. Designers have found many different ways of positioning themselves, through varying levels of engagement with computer simulations. Each position is technically justifiable and culturally palatable in its own way, within the system of relationships in which it is defined. When individuals adopt or reject these new technologies, they are not only thinking about what the technologies do for them, in an instrumental sense: they are weighing the implications for their professional relationships. Managing their relationships through simulations can put practitioners in positions of control.

Chapter 4

How do Simulations Know?

In an 1802 issue of the *Windsor Gazette*, a carpenter in New England named Asher Benjamin advertised instruction in "the art of drawing plans and elevations or any other figures perspectively."[144] Beginning in the mid-eighteenth century, drawing was a lure into formal education for young American carpenters, joiners, and other building craftsmen.[145] Interest in drawing was driven in New England by a market for the complex architectural features of English neoclassical architecture. Classical orders, circular staircases, and round- or oval-planned rooms with vaulted ceilings defied simple specification by written instructions or references to existing structures. Early instruction in drafting and descriptive geometry promised craftsmen the ability to envisage complex forms, to transmit the details of their construction, and to compete for financial gain and social mobility. In architecture's transition from craft to profession, drawing played a crucial role. It became the means by which expert knowledge, the basis of professional claims, was developed, transmitted, and maintained.[146] Today, in 2012, computer simulations are at the center of debates about what constitutes expert knowledge and how it can be managed in architecture.

Since Benjamin's time, the complexity of architecture has continued to escalate. Markets for cavernous interior spaces and multi-layered curtain-wall facades are challenging the capacity of drawing to handle all the accumulated knowledge about designs. Although many designers retain drawing as a means of expressing ideas, they are adopting computer simulation as a means to validate them. In Chapter 3, I described several circumstances in which computer simulations shape new ways of being a designer, but also new ways of knowing about designs. A master architect compromises his direct experience of drawing, in order to manage more geometrically elaborate designs through an apprentice with skills in geometric modeling. An acoustician trades the measured certainty of numerical optimization for the broad public assurance of consensus when he engages the more accessible technology of aural renderings. A structural engineer still connects with

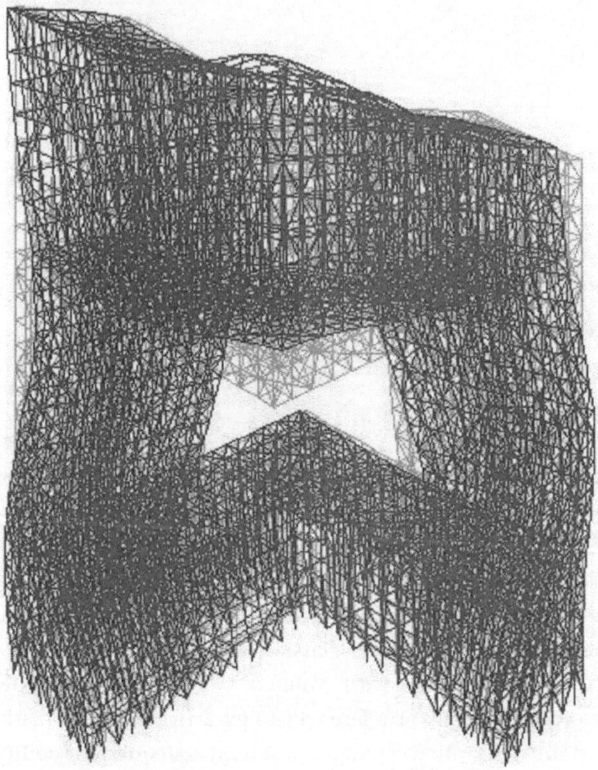

Figure 13
China Central Television (CCTV) structural simulation, performed by Arup.

collaborators through drawing, but confirms his complex designs through finite element analysis. A fire safety engineer challenges prescriptive knowledge when she uses simulations to overturn existing building regulations. In each case, computer simulations challenge the traditional basis of design knowledge.

New forms of knowledge are accepted when they establish trustworthy relationships among people and things. Drawing put Benjamin's students at a new distance from their craft, but it allowed them literally to see the work that had to be done and communicate the necessary steps to others. American building craftsmen saw drawing as a means of placing themselves in more strategic relationships with building materials, collaborators, and clients. Similarly, designers adopt computer simulations today to connect with resources and people in advantageous ways. In this chapter, I will examine some of the socio-technical contexts in which computer simulations are vetted by generalist architects and specialist engineers. Simulations are never unconditionally true or false. They must work within social systems of knowledge that include personal, complementary, and competing ways of representing and thinking about architecture.

Whither the Generalist?

Despite the rapid growth of specializations, many architects in the United States maintain that they are "generalists." Today, this means that architects try to reconcile the dispersed knowledge of many specialized designers. Architects are using computers to help manage this process of integration.[147] Ralph Jerome Architects, a 100-person office on the West Coast of the United States, uses CATIA, the computer modeling software, to realize complex projects that require it to manage the knowledge of many partnering disciplines. Here, CATIA serves as a "place" where many different kinds of knowledge meet, and where the details of construction are often contributed by consultants and fabricators. CATIA brings together knowledge of construction materials from outside collaborators with schematic information about designs.

Ralph Jerome emphasizes that for him, this technology brings the architect closer to the craftsperson who will actually handle the materials of construction. He sees CATIA as a way to bypass the many layers between sketch and final building. However, at Ralph Jerome Architects, the reconfiguration of work around CATIA has also led to confusion, redundancy, and loss of data, problems that are common when working with digital files. These developments have prompted the establishment of a new role. Like Paul Morris, Ralph Jerome needs a "keeper of the geometry," someone to play a role similar to, but more powerful than, that of Robert Laird. At Ralph Jerome's firm, this role has a formal title, "director of computing."

Malcolm Dietrich holds this role and is responsible for coordinating the geometric modeling work in the office. For Dietrich, the computer is on its way to becoming the unifying collaborative space for designers. In Dietrich's vision, one person is at the center of the building process: that person's power comes from access to knowledge, all of which is in the computer. Dietrich describes this person as a "master techie-enabled architect sitting in the middle."[148] As Dietrich envisages it, the techie-enabled architect has the potential to crystallize a new kind of integration among members of the firm and external contractors. The techie-enabled architect understands every bolt in the building and can see and coordinate the work of every person involved. Dietrich looks forward to the day when he will be able to say, "I understand what this shape is and how it's built and how pieces go together and I can validate and I can stand up and say this thing will work." On one level, the architect at the center is all-powerful; yet there is a paradox in Dietrich's vision. In this model, craftspeople are given a more creative role in design and sometimes Dietrich talks about himself as "just stitching the bits together." Being in control of the machine can seem like low-level work. "Sometimes I feel I'm just a full-time translator."

There are elements of Dietrich's vision that already are at work at Ralph Jerome Architects. For example, Dimitri Kabel, an architect at the firm, "captures" in CATIA the specific physical knowledge that fabricators bring to the design process. For Kabel, working with computer simulation has made him see the whole of architecture as being about simulation, something that was not clear to him when representations were done with pencil and paper. When a project needs special technical knowledge about a suspended glass wall, Kabel works with a curtain wall consultant to model this knowledge in CATIA; the geometric model serves as a communications medium within the office. Yet, when the consultant is asked, for example, to codify his conventions for working with glass, the current limitations of Dietrich's vision become clear. The process of fabricating this curtain wall cannot yet be described in a form that can be modeled in CATIA. Dietrich laments that "one of the hardest things is going to a fabricator and telling them, provide us with your rules; what are the rules that we need to adhere to [to] make this thing buildable?"

This example illustrates how designers use simulations to think about knowledge in architecture: its properties, its extents, and its limits. What can designers know? What can be captured and integrated through simulation? What might be lost in the process? For the foreseeable future, these questions will remain unsettled. Computer simulations are still tested every day. They must compete to gain acceptance among many more traditional ways of knowing, including personal intuition, physical mock-ups, and government regulations. In the remainder of this chapter, I will examine how simulations know in specialized realms of architecture, and examine the related problem of integration.

Specialized Systems of Knowledge

> To say that the definition of failure of structures in fire is "complex" is a huge understatement. It is much more than that, beginning right from the most elementary issue of "what kind of failure" it is that one is trying to define. As the fire safety of a structure is of interest not only to the architect and structural engineer but also to fire safety engineers and regulators/building control officers, not to mention the owner/client. It is the highly varying perspectives of this group of people that confuses [sic] the issue and makes [sic] it very difficult for a consensus on the definition of failure to emerge, if it were indeed possible.[149]

Many concerns coexist and compete for a place in building design. The difficulty of defining "failure" in the case of a building fire illustrates this well. Structural engineers define failure as the circumstances under which a building will no longer support dead and live loads. Fire safety engineers have more fragile concerns; they consider a failure to have occurred when there is a breach of compartmentation and an uncontrolled spread of smoke and flames. Owners may see failure in economic, not material terms: what are the losses incurred by the fire, including the costs of repairs and effects on productivity and business? All these positions are valid, but each suggests a very different understanding of the building in distress. Structural engineers, fire safety engineers, and owners are distinct social groups at work in building design, sometimes in collaboration, sometimes at odds, but each with an interest in defining not only failure, but what it means to know in design. For, as David Bloor elegantly summarizes, knowledge is no more than "the beliefs which people confidently hold to and live by."[150] Knowledge is not limited to truth; it is taken to mean different things by different social groups. The concerns present in the above statement from fire safety engineers at Arup suggest that design involves many social groups, each with its own requirements for knowledge. This is the context in which new technologies must gain acceptance. If we are to understand how computer simulations know in the practice of design, we must examine the varied social systems of knowledge in which they are tested.

Reflecting on the practice of simulation, designers explain the uncertainties they face and how they are resolved among colleagues, collaborators, competitors, clients, and regulators. Designers' accounts reveal that simulations are put on trial in similar ways across a variety of domains from fire safety to sustainability. First, the knowledge of computer simulations must be expected; the results of any simulation are assessed in the context of personal experience and intuition. Second, uncertainties must be made explicit by allowing that a series of possible simulation results may be true. Third, these results must be reconciled with competing assessments from other simulations, models, and experiments, as well as more holistic conceptions of good design. Finally, after simulations have passed all tests of their inherent uncertainty, they must be measured against institutionalized norms in the form of legally sanctioned ways of knowing; why should simulations be trusted over age-old regulations?

Computer simulations are never true in an absolute sense, but they can become valid for a particular audience when framed appropriately, within systems of knowledge that are both socially and technologically constructed. Furthermore, the stakes for accepting simulation go beyond due diligence. The production and operation of computer simulations in architecture is part of an ongoing ideological and professional struggle to define the state of knowledge in the field, as well as the social roles and relationships that legitimize claims to professional authority and expertise.

Expectations and Limitations

"You cannot rely on simulations. You have to understand the basis of it, you have to be able to make intuitive judgments," says Mathew Webb, a veteran in Arup's Building Engineering Group who has worked at the firm for almost 30 years.[151] Experienced engineers like Webb know that buildings are dynamic and that a static picture of how a building works should not be mistaken for reality. Simulations merely give an indication upon which design decisions can be based. "All modeling is simply confirming one's intuition," says Webb, but he is quick to soften this claim. "Although this is not entirely true, we do know what we need it to look like." Webb's comments suggest that if simulations are to avoid being rejected outright, they must first conform to the personal expectations of their operators.

However, there can be a tension between maintaining old expectations and allowing for new discoveries. Andrew Werner, of Arup's Environmental Physics Group, struggles with this tension in his use of computational fluid dynamics to predict temperature fluctuations in buildings. Even Werner, a self-acknowledged simulations expert, concedes that in most cases, a computer simulation is just a verification of what he already knows from simply looking at traditional plans and sections of a proposed building.[152] He uses computer simulations to refine initial guesses and to define, by degree, how a design diverges from standards for environmental comfort. It is only in rare instances that simulations reveal something counter-intuitive for him. Recently, Werner published a study with unusual results about the classic UK office building, a structure typically defined by abundant glazing and large internal heat gains from equipment and people.[153] Such buildings need an enormous amount of cooling. High performance glazing types portend the improvement of the thermal performance of offices, reducing the amount of cooling needed. Werner's paper announces a counter-intuitive dynamic revealed by his computer simulations, that this glazing can also trap heat in the building, leading to larger gains. But among the most experienced practitioners at Arup, such cases are seen as the exception to the rule. Werner's work on unexpected heating loads in glass enclosed offices is at the outer edge of design knowledge. Most designers take a more conservative approach; simulations must conform to their personal expectations if they are to be believed. But expectations are transient. Not all engineers share the same training, experience, and judgment.

By definition, personal knowledge differs within any group of practitioners. These differences create social divisions; for example, between generations. Across disciplines, the seductive quality of computer simulations is a subject of much distress among an older generation of practitioners.[154] Webb's earlier assertions point to long-standing concerns at Arup that simulations, particularly those done on a computer, may be given too much weight, that they may come to dominate design. Webb is part of an older generation of engineers who came of age without the support of computer simulations; today's novice engineers sometimes know little else. Halden Harrison says that there is a dangerous assumption on the part of young practitioners that if you can build it in the computer, then you can build it on site. "You have to develop an intuition about these things before you can use the computer. Young engineers need to go out and learn construction techniques." Harrison contrasts the contingent and easy experience gained through simulation with the concrete, hard-earned experience of the construction site. In Harrison's era, you had to spend a year as a builder after graduating from engineering school. Today, new graduates spend six weeks on average.[155] Harrison believes that young engineers need more hands-on training to understand how pieces go together in construction. All the great structural designers, including Pier Luigi Nervi and Jean Prouvé, understood how forms went together, reminisces Harrison. His engineering heroes from the past developed experience on the construction site in addition to developing their analytical abilities. Knowledge gained through simulation is supplemental knowledge for Harrison, not a replacement for a lifetime of on-site experience.

For Harrison, as for many designers, simulation and personal experience are two different kinds of knowledge and should support one another. But more importantly, each of these ways of knowing puts the other in relief. Designers strongly believe that knowledge absorbed on the screen is not the same as knowledge obtained on the construction site. This juxtaposition calls into question the limitations of each, because neither perspective sees all. What happens when the complexity of building designs exceeds designers' experience and ability to reason intuitively? Will new associations of people and computers ever allow design to move beyond intuition? What are the implications for how we see the role of human judgment and expertise, and the corresponding value and identity of designers? For now, these questions remain unresolved. The knowledge of computer simulations is still closely linked to the limits of personal knowledge. Understanding how computer simulations know requires an appreciation of individual histories and professional differences. Personal identities and uncertainties are ever present in the development, presentation, and validation of new technologies.

One Simulation, Many Possible Realities

Engineers use simulations not merely to confirm their own deeply held beliefs, but to exchange knowledge with many types of professional partners: architects, developers, insurers, and building regulators, to name a few. One of the ways that these designers temper the uncertain results of simulations is by allowing for the possibility that a range of outcomes could occur. In each professional interaction, designers separate questions about the basic veracity of simulations from questions about their validity. Veracity is a matter of science; validity is a problem of broader cultural acceptance.[156] Simulations may have veracity if they are based on seemingly stable scientific premises, but if their results do not conform to the assumptions and expectations of audiences, they will almost certainly be disregarded. Simulations must be bridges; they must conform to all the tenets of science and all the needs of clients. This often means acknowledging that one simulation may allow for many possible realities.

On a typical day in the New York offices of Arup, Adrian Ball, a young American engineer in the Fire Group, states emphatically that he is not doing science. He calls the knowledge about fire safety that he brings to clients and collaborators simply "common sense." His sense of self reflects the fact that fire safety algorithms and software are typically not developed in-house at Arup. As such, Ball's expertise lies in validation, determining how the science of fire safety produced elsewhere can be applied in new contexts, to suit the needs of clients, collaborators, and regulators. Debates about the validity of simulations in the Fire Group typically concern input assumptions. These assumptions are the common-sense notions that Ball uses to make science relevant for the particular concerns of his audiences.

Many assumptions that go into a simulation lie outside of the purview of science.[157] Some have to do with anticipating the material life of buildings and their changing physical properties and environments. Traditionally, these are the issues that engineers are trained to attend to. For instance, members of the Arup Fire Group often debate and tinker with the variables that represent different types of flammable materials in a proposed building. These variables and whether they are likely to change are some of the conditions used to predict the dynamics of fires in buildings. In the hypothetical case of a museum, the contents of the building could be expected to change with each exhibition. For instance, a show featuring small paintings behind glass, and another featuring large wooden sculptures pose different risks. In the rail industry, there are equally difficult problems of determining what inputs to use. Rail vehicles vary immensely in size, materials, fuel, and trigger points. Designers must rely on available information and their own experience to make assumptions about these variables.

Outside of material variables are other, more intangible concerns. Foremost among these are assumptions about the behavior and experience of humans living and working in buildings. Often these variables are standardized or integrated into regulations and go unchallenged. Often practitioners lack methods for tracking or projecting human behavior. However, this situation is changing. Talcott Saunders, one of Ball's colleagues at the Arup Fire Group, explains that the most recent controversies in his group have been over technologies for simulating evacuation, the behavior of people in a fire. Despite some early successes, Arup fire safety engineers remain skeptical about the models of human behavior in their simulations. Saunders is exhibiting understandable caution when he says, "You can't get it spot on with these models. I'm still not convinced that these models are worth the investment. It is easier to model smoke from a fire than anything to do with people."[158]

Despite similar concerns throughout design, in an increasing number of technical domains, designers are considering assumptions about human experience as something that might be interrogated through computer simulations. Haden Bailey, an architect and engineer working on issues of sustainability at Arup, is concerned with the assumptions about human behavior built into representations of energy use in buildings. He focuses on seemingly simple issues, such as how the inhabitants of buildings operate its windows and doors. Inhabitants may draw the shades, for example, when it is too sunny. That is fine, as long as they do not turn on the lights as well. When designers run lighting and energy simulations, they often assume that people act rationally, that they do not commit blatant energy-use errors. Typical computer simulations may also overlook extra appliances like space heaters and fans that people bring into buildings to change their environment. A considerable amount of Bailey's time is spent thinking about humans, not building systems. "One of the hardest things to do is predict the energy use in buildings," says Bailey.[159] The tools for assessing both human perceptions and responses are not there yet. Bailey tries to contain the uncertainties of human behavior in buildings, by summing them up as merely "the question of human interface." But what are buildings beyond an interface between humans and an often inhospitable environment? Uncertain models of human behavior threaten the basic legitimacy of knowledge generated through computer simulations.

Arup practitioners sometimes get around these uncertainties by developing simulations, not in the pursuit of absolute truth, but rather as a response to the assumptions and expectations of their audiences. For instance, the simulation produced for a governmental compliance check might differ from the simulation produced for a developer, or an insurer. Governmental compliance expectations are often standardized, but they may be too conservative from the point of view of developers, who try to anticipate not only short-term uses of a building, but the use patterns of future inhabitants, a process called "future proofing." Meanwhile, insurers are probably the most conservative audience. According to Bailey, insurers "demand to look at the worst case scenario."

Designers typically respond by simulating multiple outcomes: some satisfy local governments; some please clients; others appease insurers. These iterations form a context of evaluation, which helps to separate questions about the basic veracity of a computer simulation from questions about assumptions and expectations. A meaningful simulation, argues Christopher Huang, a young mechanical engineer at Arup, is one that involves many iterations over various assumptions and designs. From this set of iterations, practitioners can identify not only designs that are optimal, but also those that are most cost effective in context.

One of the dangers of computer simulations is that by varying the assumptions, one can show nearly any result. This is what historian and engineer David Mindell means when he says that computer simulations may be "doomed to succeed."[160] Given the inherent malleability of computer simulations, how do designers reassure themselves, as well as clients, collaborators, and regulators, of the reliability of their results? Dealing with this problem requires designers to show their results in the context of standardized expectations of building performance. From Huang's perspective, the results of a computer simulation can only be judged against a baseline of acceptability. Establishing this baseline is Arup's way of demonstrating the relative improvement of an innovative design over a typical one. Without a baseline, there is no shared understanding of which designs are acceptable or improved. Unfortunately, establishing a baseline is non-trivial, particularly in the case of fire safety. Only in the last several years have designers identified the lack of fire safety criteria as a research need. As such, there is a shortage of consistent data about fire and human behavior in fires, in part because of the dangers involved in generating this data experimentally. There are few guidelines to define what an acceptable safety risk is on a given project. Validating computer simulations for fire safety is still an open problem.

The premises of simulations – the underlying building science and algorithms – are largely developed outside of practice, in government and academic laboratories. Designers must worry about how to bridge the findings of these institutions and the needs of audiences in order to render simulations valid. Their scattershot approach, conceding that many different measures of building performance are possible, is an attempt to make uncertainties explicit. Computer simulations can know various outcomes. The uncertainties of human behavior and the unforeseeable changes in buildings and their environments over a lifetime make virtual views into the future of building performance blurry at best. As a result, many possibilities must be designed for.

Simulations in Competition

I have explained how a range of outcomes from one computer simulation can be used to give context to individual results; similarly, a range of simulations are used to validate one another. Indeed, computer simulations with different underlying premises should be compared. Christopher Huang explains that there is a lack of confidence in any one simulation, a frustration that "the tools aren't good enough."[161] Echoing an earlier theme, Huang also discusses the danger that "people think they know what's going to happen and they correct their simulation accordingly." This error is less likely to go unnoticed when several simulations must be made to correspond. There is still a lot of debate over what constitutes a good computer simulation and how each might be independently validated. Without other measures to back it up, there is little desire among designers to trust one computer simulation alone.

The Arup Fire Group works with a suite of simulations. In most projects, they work their way up to advanced computer simulations, like computational fluid dynamics models (CFDs), which can be time-intensive and expensive. These are often held in reserve. Adrian Ball's initial advice to architects is often arrived at through hand calculations, which might be thought of as simple simulations. There are numerous intermediary techniques between a hand calculation and the use of advanced computer simulations. Spreadsheets are akin to automated hand calculations, used to handle a diverse array of issues including smoke management, heat, materials, egress, and the placement of smoke detectors and alarms. Zone models, which are slightly more sophisticated, divide a room into heat and smoke zones. CFD models are among the highest resolution and most nuanced methods that fire safety engineers have for calculating smoke flows. However, they are just one of a host of techniques for simulating fires which are used to inform one another.

When practitioners at Arup must choose between multiple possible simulation techniques, it is the particular needs of their audiences that guide decisions. For example, the client for a transportation center at Washington Dulles International Airport in the United States hired Arup to design a glass enclosure for an underground train. The client specified that the enclosure should hold up under severe heat – the heat of a train on fire – for two minutes. The pre-engineered fire safety system proposed by Arup was only guaranteed for 20 seconds. Testing the system beyond 20 seconds was difficult to undertake computationally, in particular because the glass could shatter and complicate the dynamics of the fire. Arup instead built a physical simulation, in order to show that the safety system could behave to the specifications of the client. In many cases, physical tests cannot be pursued in-house at Arup because of their expense. This is particularly true in the area of fire safety. Often fire safety engineers access physical testing through relationships with universities or government research laboratories. However, physical tests can go wrong just as easily as their virtual counterparts. After all, as isolated pieces of a larger architectural system, physical tests require numerous simplifications, assumptions, and abstractions to appear valid outside the context of the whole.

Often designers compare the results of multiple simulations, performed in different media. Haden Bailey, the sustainability expert, explains that none of these simulations are completely reliable, but seeing whether they correspond can be useful. One of the early buildings in which Bailey combined several simulations was the Inland Revenue building, a 40,000 square meter office completed in 1991 in Nottingham, UK. The architect on the project was Michael Hopkins. During an initial meeting with Hopkins, Bailey suggested that the building should be designed to eliminate the need for mechanical systems. The mechanical systems were anticipated to push the budget over its limit.

As an alternative, Bailey proposed a passive airflow system, a novel suggestion at the time for such a large building. Bailey and his team suggested tall ventilation towers that would draw air through the building using a phenomenon known as the "stack effect." These towers would generate air circulation in the building, using differences in air density due to temperature and moisture variations along their height. The client was concerned that air would not ascend the towers with enough speed to generate adequate ventilation. In response, Bailey and his team added fans to the scheme to draw the air up by mechanical force and used a set of complementary simulations to convince the client of the system's feasibility.

The team used three separate simulation techniques to verify the design. First, finite element analysis was used to simulate the network of heat flows, but not airflow. A second CFD simulation was used to add airflow analysis. These two computer simulations were combined. Finally, a third simulation, a physical test, was done at Cambridge University. The university used "salt bath testing," a means of representing fluid dynamics by analyzing the dispersion of salt as it is dropped into a vat of water. The resulting plume is videotaped and the video is turned upside down so that the vat resembles a room with ventilation at floor level. This final test gave engineers and clients a counterpoint to the predictions of the two computational simulations. Of course, all of these techniques are simplified representations, all flawed in one way or another. They were found to be fairly consistent though, enough to prove their point. It is important to note that even a physical test, like the salt bath test, is not reliable on its own. There is no ground for truth in simulation. The best one can hope for is a good correspondence between simulations generated in a number of ways.

Any one simulation may never give a complete representation of a building, but it can gain value when strategically juxtaposed to alternatives. Arup practitioners often define their simulations against those of their competitors. This is nowhere more apparent than in the area of lighting design. "There are many competing programs for lighting simulation out there right now. None of them have the level of confidence that we have in Radiance," says Michael Cullen, a lighting designer working in the London offices of Arup.[162] In contrast, Cullen classifies the lighting simulations in 3D Studio Max, a program typically used by architects, as "fake."[163] The 3D Studio Max program is marketed as an illustration device; it is meant to be an instrument for artists, not a scientific or engineering tool. "It doesn't have the physical accuracy of Radiance," says Cullen. "You wouldn't be able to simulate the particular type of lamp." The details of the lamp design and its environment are all highly tunable in Radiance, but less so in 3D Studio Max. The core difference, says Cullen, is the way Radiance handles inter-reflections in a process called backward ray tracing. But perhaps just as important is the way such simulations are enlisted differently by engineers and architects. Cullen dismisses the results of 3D Studio Max by explaining how architects use the software to create virtual lighting solutions that are effective for their own representational purposes, but physically impractical, like placing a single light source 1,000 feet in the air. Simulations are not merely made to correspond with one another; they also gain legitimacy in the context of strong competition with other technologies and their operators.

Figure 14 Realtime simulation of a hospital interior.

Total Simulation

Simulations are not only brought together in juxtaposition. The union of two or more specialized simulations can be complementary, an attempt to form a more holistic perspective on building performance.[164] Realtime is an immersive application developed by Arup to integrate multiple simulations. Here simulations are not held up against one another; they are superimposed in a virtual reality setting. Clemens Atkinson, an architect and researcher in Arup's Foresight, Innovation and Incubation Group runs the project. Atkinson demonstrates a "Realtime" train station, developed by Arup in conjunction with the British architects at Foster and Partners. "Look how long it takes us to walk the entire length of the train platform," says Atkinson.[165] "That's one surprising thing we never would have known, had we not built this model." In Realtime, you can experience the space of the station with acoustical treatment and lighting effects; you can see visualizations of structural forces, airflow, or temperature mapped onto the virtual surfaces of the space; the software even displays simulated inhabitants. Realtime is the closest thing Arup has to a comprehensive tool for building simulation. Adrian Ball's group is currently working on an ambitious project with Realtime to capture the experience of being trapped in a burning building, incorporating people, fire, smoke, structure, sound, and lighting. The ambitious fire safety engineer believes that, despite disciplinary differences, there are enough areas of overlap to make this integration work. There will always be a delegation of tasks, argues Ball, but engineers share a core of knowledge that allows them to understand other disciplines in principle and integrate their efforts. Realtime is the platform at Arup that wants to allow such integration to occur.

However, Realtime is not yet a reality; problems abound. The computational fluid dynamics map is pixilated. There are limits to the resolution of such analysis, says Atkinson. There are also still difficulties aligning all the simulations. Realtime uses slightly different geometric models to generate each one. In one example, the lighting analysis does not line up with the floor plates. Although the mismatch is subtle, it is noticeable, particularly by domain experts. A director at Arup easily noticed it during one of Atkinson's presentations. Pierre Moreau, an engineer working in the Advanced Geometry Unit, wrote much of the code for Realtime. "I am the salesperson and Pierre is the technical person," explains Atkinson. Atkinson and Moreau's Realtime is a context in which many, otherwise independent, ways of knowing about a building can be woven together into one experience, accessible to engineers, architects, and clients alike. We see here not just a technical solution, but a prescription for how social groups in design should coordinate their activities, with unstated assumptions about the nature of their demands on representations of knowledge.

Realtime is one of the strategies in place at Arup for addressing the rampant problems of specialization. Thirty years ago, Ove Arup, the firm's founder was already warning, "we are drowning in specialization." He championed a holistic approach to design, which he named "total architecture" after the early twentieth-century manifesto written by Bauhaus director Walter Gropius.[166] Ove Arup's passion for total architecture is documented in his papers, speeches, and business initiatives, like the creation of Arup Associates, a prototype of an integrated design studio, a merger of architectural and engineering working styles.[167] Although the firm's aspiration toward total architecture endures, it has continued to diversify and specialize. Julian Butler, an engineer working in the Lighting Group at Arup, expresses his personal concerns about specialization. "As we specialize . . . as we produce new organizations . . . it will be harder to produce holistic design. Who will be the integrator?" Butler sees this as a job for the generalist designer. In America, this has traditionally been the role of the architect. Today, in 2012, an increasing number of designers, such as Atkinson, are suggesting that technology, perhaps his project Realtime, can take on this disputed role.

However, in spite of their aspirations for total architecture, many designers at Arup are doubtful about placing technology at the center of design, and wary of the benefits of conflating different types of simulation. Butler has concerns about the effects of specialization, but has yet to be convinced by Realtime. He sees Atkinson's models as superficial, merely "technical demonstrations." "I'm skeptical about the single model environment," says Butler. He explains that buildings need to be abstracted in different ways depending on what your interest is. For example, in an integrated lighting and airflow model, the needs for particular refinements are not necessarily consistent or complementary. If a wall has an air-supply register that is set back, the dimension of the slot is very important for airflow, but hardly important at all for lighting. Likewise, mullion design is an important detail for lighting, but it may have very little effect on airflow or, to add in another dimension, acoustics. Too many details in a single simulation will limit its speed and divert the focus from any one design problem. Butler explains that Realtime whitewashes the purposeful, nuanced differences and distances that have accompanied specialization. "We are all interested in different things. We work at different times. Integrated simulations are not an enormous design help." Closing the gaps between specialized simulations raises significant social concerns. How will designers reconcile the outcomes of independent simulations? Who will be at the center? If we look at software as an embodiment of the knowledge and judgment of its human developers, we might see Realtime not simply as a technological solution, but as a solution that gives the center to human technologists like Atkinson and Moreau.

Disagreements about the role of technology in achieving total architecture proliferate. Bailey, who studied both architecture and engineering, has been a champion of integrated design since his earliest days at the firm. His current position in Arup's Building Sustainability Group is increasingly about enabling collaboration and integration. Bailey has learned that if integrated design is to happen, the impetus must come from people. "To date, I've not seen the computer being a leading component of integrated design. A database doesn't produce integrated design. Many a designer is just working his layers of the database, without concern for other disciplines." In other words, computer simulations cannot force integration; people must cross boundaries, they must care. As Bailey explains, "there has to be a change in the attitudes of individuals. They have to see the benefit of integrated design." Bailey is not alone in his apprehension about the ability of technology to bring people together. Acoustician Linus Russell says the type of integration suggested by total architecture does not come along with computer simulations as such: "Individuals must create this symbiosis." Edward Malone, a member of the Facade Group says, "Arup is still a series of silos. The thing is to be aware of the silo next to you."[168] Malone asserts that Arup's most severe competitors are architects who do the engineering themselves and potentially do a better job at design integration. However, some of the most technical designers at Arup see architects losing this ability. "There used to be a master builder, but that no longer is the case," says Andrew Werner. As knowledge becomes increasingly performance-based, architects will have more trouble integrating diverse areas of knowledge in design. How can architects evaluate integrated simulations, if each simulation is a black box and the misalignments between them are not easily visible? Do computer simulations make it more difficult for architects to take the center?

In Arup's struggle to make a place for itself among a system of professions and simulations in architecture, integration is more than the philosophy of total architecture; it is a competitive strategy. According to Malone, Arup is on the leading edge of consultancies because of its ability, however impaired, to "put things together." He asserts that what Arup can bring to the table, beyond what other specialist consultants bring, is "true integration," by which he means the established personal relationships within the organization. Malone has acknowledged that there are gaps, but technology may yet play a role in helping Arup to bridge those gaps. Right now, says Malone, that kind of technology is missing because there is no central building model. The only common denominator between simulations is geometry. Realtime has intentions of becoming a central model, with implications for how practitioners at Arup work together, collaborate and compete with architects, and interface with clients. Integration is both a technical problem and a social one.

Atkinson and Moreau are still trying to get Realtime running as a lucrative business, a new product that Arup can sell to a variety of clients. The two have already won quite a few contracts, but have not yet convinced Arup to put in the funds for a virtual reality set-up that will cost one million pounds sterling. "[Realtime] is in a period of incubation," explains Atkinson. Only time will tell whether Realtime can gain the broad social acceptance it needs to become a system for knowledge management. It is one of many technological efforts in architecture to redefine design knowledge in relation to computer simulation for both ideological and strategic ends.[169]

Regulating Simulations

Beyond the internal uncertainties of computer simulation lie institutionalized and legally sanctioned conceptions of design knowledge, obstacles to new ways of thinking about buildings and arranging the social organization of design work. How do computer simulations overturn culturally and politically embedded knowledge bureaucracies? Behind the use of computer simulations at the regulatory level is a conceptual differentiation between two ways of knowing: scrutinizing a design to make sure it follows established regulations; and virtually experiencing the building before it is built.

Amelia Pearce, of the Arup Fire Group, began to question standardized approaches to fire protection as far back as the early 1970s. Why separate fire safety considerations from structural design? Applying fire-resistant paint and sprinkler systems to an a priori structural scheme is inefficient. Pearce worked for years at the Fire Research Station near London, developing regulations herself, based on experiments and simple mathematical models (see Chapter 2). It was not until after she was hired by Arup and began to work on actual building projects that she realized a limitation in these regulations. Today, in 2012, fire safety is still widely enforced by the building regulations that Pearce helped to develop. She is retired now, but Talcott Saunders, a current member of the Arup Fire Group, has made her mission to challenge building regulations into a business.[170] Saunders identifies building regulations as an outmoded way of knowing. They represent what Saunders calls a "prescriptive" approach to design. In contrast, he champions a "performance-based" approach, the contingent but exploratory conception of knowledge that computer simulations offer.

Saunders' distinction between prescriptive and performance-based ways of knowing in design is symptomatic of an effort by practitioners across architecture to situate new knowledge among traditional ways of knowing. Amelia Pearce explains this strategy: "You move backwards and forwards from what they know, from regulations, to what you are proposing." Engineers are often in the business of negotiating or "finding alternatives to achieve the intent of regulations."[171] When designers confront regulators with new computer simulations, they enter into what Saunders calls a "bargaining area." In this shared space of alternatives, computer simulations come up against highly institutionalized forms of knowledge encoded in building regulations.

When Saunders' team issues a report to the local regulators, it rarely goes through without an intensive period of questioning. Regulators ask the group to present alternatives and variations and later to follow up on unanswered questions. Computer simulations become rhetorical tools, the focus for an iterative process in which they are adjusted to suit the concerns of their audience. Amelia Pearce is particularly sensitive to the needs of such audiences. "It is important that you try to explain your results. Pictures and diagrams are important," says Pearce. Engineers put new knowledge in context with what regulators already know. The work of Saunders and Pearce requires them to move from the science, to the propositions of their colleagues and clients, to the needs of building regulators. In creating a good simulation, Pearce offers this advice: "[Y]ou relate it to what they know and are happy with." But simulations are not always successful with building regulators. Arup is still learning how to tailor its simulations for authorities in different regulatory climates. In order to create a role globally, practitioners must learn to see simulations through a cultural lens, conforming not simply to their own personal expectations, but to the needs of a diverse range of audiences.

Design involves the negotiation of many social groups, each with its own demands on representations of knowledge. Each social relationship puts simulations in tension in different ways. Even in a group as small as Arup Fire, there can be as many ways of knowing as there are types of professional relationships. The group retains its authority and the validity of its simulations by understanding and maintaining these relationships. In the preceding accounts, designers explain how they resolve the uncertainties inherent in building simulations, in coordination with colleagues, collaborators, competitors, clients, and regulators. Across a range of domains, these accounts illustrate how computer simulations know in different social and technological contexts: personal, organizational, disciplinary, strategic, and institutional. Building simulations are never true, but they can be accepted by audiences when adequately situated within socially defined systems of knowledge. While contributing new material understandings and expanding the range of designs that can become buildings, computer simulations also carry unanswered questions. They call attention to the limits of human intuition and reveal doubts about the appropriate organization of design work, including who or what (if anything) can bring together divergent ways of knowing in design.

Chapter 5

Towards a Pluralistic Formalism

During the last century, the term "form" has been used primarily by architects as a means of defining their professional space.[172] The modernists placed it in opposition to other dimensions of design; it represented a consideration set apart from the function, ornamentation, and social value of architecture.[173] Today, in 2012, in the face of new technologies for simulating architecture with extraordinary precision, debates about what constitutes good form are increasingly technical. Architects are turning to technical specialists and, increasingly, turning technical themselves, to get a better handle on form through computer simulation. Questions about how computer simulations might not only redefine form, but enhance its control and complexity, are pervasive. Meanwhile, the implications of new approaches to form for the social organization of architecture are often overlooked. How are different conceptions of form reconciled among designers?

In this chapter, I discuss how designers with different disciplinary perspectives use computer simulations to define a shared space of alternatives, a literal and conceptual arena in which good form can be found. The idea for such a space originates in Herbert Simon's writings. However, Simon's mathematical account of design exploration leaves the human explorers out. We need to acknowledge that Simon's space of alternatives is a social space, in which "satisficing" designs are agreed upon by many people.[174]

In an architectural context, design alternatives develop within spaces of interdisciplinary interaction. Recognizing these spaces is one step toward a pluralistic formalism.[175] A pluralistic approach to form challenges the autonomy of individual authors. It acknowledges the multiple ways of articulating form in architecture, each with its own personal or disciplinary history and associated methods of simulation. Pluralism can help us broaden the definition of design, to include the form-making work of both architects and engineers, as well as other participants from contractors to policy makers, not explored at length here, but important to understanding form in all its

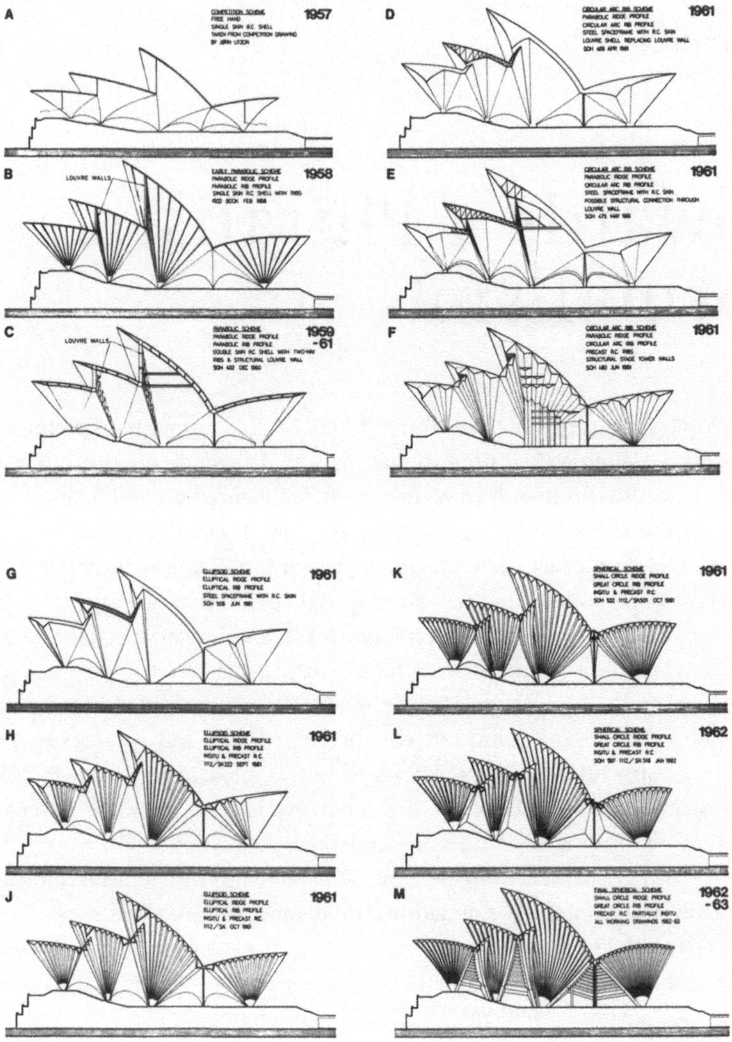

Figure 15
Variations in the form of the Sydney Opera House roofs, from the competition proposal to the spherical solution.

dimensions. This is not the first call for pluralism in design, nor is this an exhaustive exploration of the concept.[176] I am interested in characterizing the kind of pluralistic formalism that can develop around computer simulations.

Personal Form

In order to understand some of the dimensions of changing attitudes toward form, let us return to the architecture office of Paul Morris Associates to see the distinctly personal aspects of form-making at work. When Drew Thorndike produces a new geometric model of a library with AutoCAD, it has different formal qualities than the original model in Rhino (see Chapter 2). He explains[177] that repetition and flat surfaces make the design easier to build virtually in AutoCAD, but also simpler to construct physically. The warped surfaces used in the Rhino model would be very expensive to fabricate, especially in glass. Furthermore, Thorndike's real expertise is in AutoCAD, not Rhino. His decision to switch from Rhino to AutoCAD is both a formal decision and a professional bias. In order to translate the design into AutoCAD, the Rhino model has to be recast into a new geometry. In other words, the latest version of the building is not just shaped in AutoCAD, it is shaped for AutoCAD. Thorndike describes the geometric space of AutoCAD as "platonic" and Rhino as "warped." Although this is not satisfying as a technical description of the two virtual workspaces, for Thorndike it serves to differentiate them conceptually. While AutoCAD's geometry might not be literally platonic, limited to the set of regular convex polyhedrons, it is certainly more constrained than Rhino, which uses NURBS to describe complex curves and surfaces with much more flexibility and precision.[178] Thorndike's choice of software, although motivated by a personal understanding rather than a deep technical one, starts to shape a space of alternatives.

His decision to use AutoCAD is as much about preserving his creative role in the project as it is about making a design that conforms to the firm's ideas about form and a rational use of resources. He could have asked another architect to do the work that he could not do with Rhino, but unlike his boss Morris, Thorndike is carving out his identity in the firm by working closely with computers. He says that asking others to make a model for you takes longer. He does not directly state that it makes you dependent on them, but this idea is present in everything he says:

> First of all, you have to wait for that person to become available. Then you have to explain the whole project to them. Lastly, if you want to hold their interest, you have to give them something significant to work on. I would rather do it myself.[179]

In the course of working on the library project, Thorndike improves his ability to move back and forth between warped geometries in Rhino and platonic geometries in AutoCAD. He feels strongly that learning Rhino will help him extend his role in developing competition work with Morris. Skill at geometric modeling enables him to negotiate a role in the office. It is a "chip" that provides access to certain tasks. However, he has worked in the office for 12 years and knows that, within the Paul Morris office, his role in design will only extend so far. Eventually, he wants to venture out on his own. For Thorndike, working at Paul Morris is an opportunity not only to learn about design but about the mechanics of owning a firm and managing projects.

However, Thorndike stresses that for his long-term development, non-technical skills, such as project development, may be equally or more important for him. He must continually negotiate his roles as designer, simulations expert, and manager in order to assure a creative place for himself in contemporary practice.

Thorndike's story highlights the way in which form is shaped by personal interactions between architects and their technologies. But this is only the first part of the story. As I turn to the social dimensions of form-making outside the architect's office, I also shift in focus, from personal ambitions to professional allegiances. During the twentieth century, modernist architects used the aphorism "form follows function" to define their professional association with form.[180] Architects of the modern era used drawing to connect function, what a building does, to form, what a building is. Today, in 2012, adherence to this sentiment has waned. Form does not simply follow function; the relationship between form and function is more complicated than ever. Engineers are defining form and function in technical languages and expressing their relationship in terms of simulated performance. Architects are struggling to find their own conceptions of form in collaboration and competition with engineers. Framing the problem of good form is a question of professional jurisdiction: who understands architecture, its effects, and how to control them? Structures, facade design, lighting, and acoustics are among a range of contested professional domains, all handled independently by architects a century ago, that I will examine in this chapter. Computer simulations and technical specialists have since come into play. In contemporary practice, designers negotiate control in each of these domains, trying to define new, shared spaces for work and to extend the boundaries of their own professional jurisdiction.

Disciplinary Form

One of the earliest uses of computer simulations to evaluate form at Arup is also one of the firm's best-known projects, the Sydney Opera House in New South Wales, Australia. Structural engineers at Arup established a professional place for themselves on the project by distinguishing between two conceptions of form. "It was one of those cases where the best architectural form is not the best structural form,"[181] remarked Ove Arup, upon seeing the winning entry for the design by architect Jørn Utzon. "The sails forming the roof would be difficult to construct because they did not accommodate the basic thrust lines."[182]

In 1957, Arup joined forces with Utzon's architecture firm to transform the design of the Opera House from a competition entry into a constructible building.[183] However, their collaboration was defined by their differing conceptions of form. Ove Arup and his team were concerned with structural integrity, and at the heart of this, the calculability of form. Arup

Figure 16 Early model of the Sydney Opera House under discussion. Jørn Utzon is on the left.

wrote, "The interplay of surfaces made an assessment of structural feasibility by normal approximations difficult and of dubious value."[184] Meanwhile, Utzon's team had aesthetic and expressive aspirations. "I have made a sculpture – a sculpture covering the necessary functions; in other words, the rooms express themselves, the size of the rooms is expressed in these roofs."[185]

Their interests were not necessarily contrary. However, in order for the design of the Opera House roofs to be worked on collaboratively and in order for the work to be coordinated, differing conceptions of form among Utzon's architects and Arup's engineers had to be reconciled. Despite the well-examined, long-term difficulties of the project, the successful resolution of the form of the Opera House roofs provides a useful example through which to understand how engineers use computer simulations to resolve issues of form in collaboration with architects.[186] Engineers have their own approaches to form, which they define in opposition to architectural aims. In Ove Arup's description of the Sydney Opera House roofs, he suggests that there are at least two ways of thinking about form: structural and architectural. His assertion that form can and should be evaluated by more than one standard is a way of creating a professional space for his work through a conceptual difference with architects.

Arup understood that maintaining this professional space would require translation and compromise. He wrote, "Utzon was quite willing to change his shapes in order to reduce the [structural] moments, but any major deviation from the architect's proposal would not have been the design which won the competition . . . I therefore advised him to retain his basic idea and we would somehow make it work."[187] Both Arup and Utzon wanted to find a mutually satisfying design, but they were working with different ways of representing and evaluating form. Utzon's team used drawings and wooden models. Arup's team employed a host of computational techniques, including a hybrid simulation made of strain gauges, physical weights, and a Pegasus computer used to analyze the distribution of loads.[188] Geometry became the intermediary language. A successive set of curvilinear geometries (parabolic, elliptical, and spherical) defined the shared space of alternatives through which Utzon and Arup pursued a mutually satisfying form for the opera house roofs.

A concrete expert working with Arup, Ronald Jenkins, proposed several geometrically simple structural shell solutions for the roofs.[189] Jenkins' shells were based on parabolic or ellipsoidal geometries. However, these were later excluded because they deviated too much from Utzon's original form, as described in the competition model and drawings.[190] Although the form of Jenkins' structural shells did not appeal to Utzon, he accepted the medium of geometry as a means of dealing with Arup's engineers. Even after Jenkins left the project and another of Arup's engineers, Jack Zunz, came on board, geometry remained the central medium of exchange. Zunz and Utzon struggled to find an appropriate geometric expression of Utzon's original form.

"As far as I was concerned, the [original] geometry was sacrosanct," said Zunz initially.[191] However, after repeated attempts to make Utzon's competition scheme work, the "original geometry" came to be seen as a "geometric straightjacket."[192] Zunz and his team told Utzon that the only way to create a structurally and economically responsible form was to base it on a spherical or toroidal geometry.[193] Utzon eventually reformed his shells using geometric pieces derived from a single sphere. The resulting form could be divided into repetitive ribs, ideal for analysis and construction. Utzon explained the form as a compromise between his values and the values of Arup:

> If you drop a big crystal ball on the floor and then pick up the pieces, the top face of each piece will have the same curve. This means that the pieces are in harmony with one another; they come from the same sphere with the same radius and therefore when they are built up in space, we know that they will interact according to a natural law and that the composition is in equilibrium . . . We can now divide this into identical parts like slicing an orange. These become the ribs and then the ribs can be divided up into the smaller Y-shaped segments – all having the one common curve, the radius of the ball . . . You have here the precision of mass-production with the freedom you normally have only from handmade things.[194]

Figure 17 Spherical model depicting the geometric derivation of the Sydney Opera House roof shapes.

Utzon embraced the form because of its freedom. Arup was satisfied by its precision. Although Utzon and Arup maintained their separate perspectives, they converged in a common space. Parabolic, ellipsoidal, and finally spherical geometries were the basis for a set of alternatives defined by both the model building tools of the architect and the structural calculations of the engineer. In this context, we can see such geometries as both trading zones and spaces of alternatives. Ultimately, the spherical geometry proved to be the solution space that allowed for both the architectural and the structural evaluation of form to be satisfied. For Arup, the spherical geometry represented a standardized, rational set of shapes that were calculable and thus could be made structural. For Utzon, the spherical geometry served aesthetic goals, producing a compositional harmony among the shells. Two divergent conceptions of form were expressed, negotiated, and reconciled in this way.

Figure 18 Sydney Opera House completed with spherical geometry.

Intent and Performance

Utzon's and Arup's independent conceptions of form are not simply professional affiliations; they echo a deeper philosophical division over the meaning of form. Is form abstract, an intention, or is it something known through the senses, a performance? Architectural historian Adrian Forty traces the contested meaning of form as far back as Ancient Greece.[195] He notes that Plato's writing distinguishes between "that which always is and never becomes" and "that which is always becoming but never is." The first, writes Plato in *Timaeus*, is an idea, "apprehensible by intelligence with the aid of reasoning, being eternally the same." The second is the object of sensation. Plato considered form to be unchanging and known only to the mind. He contrasts the form with the thing, which is known by sense. Plato's student, Aristotle, was reluctant to make the same sharp distinction. He wrote that "each thing itself and its essence are one and the same."[196]

What is form then? This question remains vital, and not only in the rhetoric of philosophers. Divergent conceptions of form underlie professionals' attempts to differentiate their work and claim a role for themselves within architecture. In many contemporary examples, architects claim dominion over the intent of form, while engineers profess expertise in predicting performance. However, there are also cases where the opposite is true. In either case, it is certainly a false choice. What is the mental construct, intent, without its grounding in the physical world? What is performance, without the mind to make sense of it? Upon reflection, it is hard to disagree with Aristotle; the thing and its essence are deeply entangled. However, in practice, such artificial distinctions about form continue to proliferate, allowing multiple perspectives to operate in parallel.

In the examples that follow, engineers use simulations to make new claims about the performance of form. By articulating form in new sensorial ways, simulations create alternative spaces of convergence in architecture. Designs, conceptions of design, and the distribution of design work are resolved in these spaces, if only temporarily.

As I move beyond the historical example of the Sydney Opera House roofs, I will explain how more advanced computer simulations have been used to change the way form is expressed, negotiated, and reconciled among practitioners. These technologies have opened new spaces of collaborative form-making that accommodate unanticipated social roles and relationships. The examples that follow, from the project history of Arup, focus on shared design spaces that bridge the conceptual distinction between the intent of form, attributed to architects, and its performance, an area of knowledge increasingly claimed by engineers. My characterization of this distinction, as the difference between intent and performance, is a tentative simplification on the way toward more nuanced descriptions of the professional claims made on behalf of form.

In the example of the Sydney Opera House, form was evaluated by Arup in terms of structure or forces, a performance described through a network of sensors applied to a scale model of the roofs. Arup has since expanded into numerous other areas of evaluation. Their contemporary work highlights performance in a range of disciplines. I will examine how technical specialists at Arup construct the performance of form in facade design, lighting, and acoustics through the use of computer simulations, and how they differentiate their work from the work of generalist architects in order to create shared spaces for both. My examples represent moments in recent history when computer simulations were used by practitioners to shape novel alternatives for clients and reveal new aesthetic conditions for architecture.

One example, the Wexner Center for the Arts, is a renovation project in which designers and curators faced a highly constrained space of alternatives. The intent of the building was celebrated, but performance inside was an embarrassment. The Wexner Center required modifications to the material and mechanical systems that maintained the building's temperature, humidity, and light levels. Designers at Arup put together a sophisticated suite of environmental simulations for the first time, in order to test alternate systems and imagine new sensory experiences for the building. In a second example, new construction on a Mercedes-Benz design studio, designers faced the inverse problem. The client precisely defined the performance of the form, but there was uncertainty about how to achieve it. Lighting designers made an early and unprecedented use of photorealistic lighting simulations to test the perceptual qualities of an unconventional form for the studio. Finally, the example of the Alice Tully Hall renovation illustrates how designers explored a shared space in which intent and performance could be examined in tandem using a real-time acoustical simulator. In all these examples, diverging notions of good form reflect more profound differences. With some exceptions, professional designers do not often leverage philosophical rhetoric to define their work. However, their choices about how to articulate form are both ideological and strategic. Designers are looking for ways in which they can both differentiate and connect themselves within a broader system of professions.

Preserving the Intent

Arup's renovation of the Wexner Center for the Arts, a museum in Columbus, Ohio, provides a contemporary example of an architecture project in which the shared space of alternatives was constrained by the building's unchallengeable form. The Arup Facade Group worked directly with the Wexner Center administration, but had little contact with the architect, Peter Eisenman – a well-known practitioner and academic who won a high-profile competition to design the Wexner Center, fixing the architectural form early on. Eisenman's

Figure 19 Wexner Center for the Arts interior.

original scheme was constructed in 1989. Arup was hired in 2002, when the museum closed for a three-year renovation.

Arup's relationship with the administration of the Wexner Center was defined around a formal objective, to change the environmental performance of the museum while retaining the intent of Eisenman's form. Sarah Geldin, director of the Wexner Center, explains, "This is a landmark of a kind of architectural practice at a certain point in time. We recognized the importance of preserving the architectural intent."[197] Eisenman's form, the idea behind the architecture, was considered sacrosanct. It is part of the museum's collection, says Christopher Huang, the mechanical engineer. The performance of the form was another matter: Arup's task was to alter the environmental performance fundamentally – to establish stable temperatures, lighting, and humidity in the galleries. In Arup's report to the Wexner administration, Huang explains, "The computational modeling undertaken shows that the use of a high performance curtain wall and skylight system in conjunction with a redesigned mechanical system will allow stable temperature and humidity to be maintained in the Wexner Center galleries."[198] With only minor alterations, the engineers preserved the Wexner Center's intent, primarily interpreted as its geometry, but changed the way it felt to be there.

It is not difficult to understand why the museum experienced problems maintaining a stable interior environment. From a geometric perspective, the form of the building is highly unconventional. "There were few right angles," says Huang.[199] "Eisenman's building started the wave of crazy looking art museums . . . other museums were just big boxes." Adrian Forty describes Eisenman's motivation in design as a "crusade against functionalism."[200] Using form as the "instrument of attack," Eisenman designed

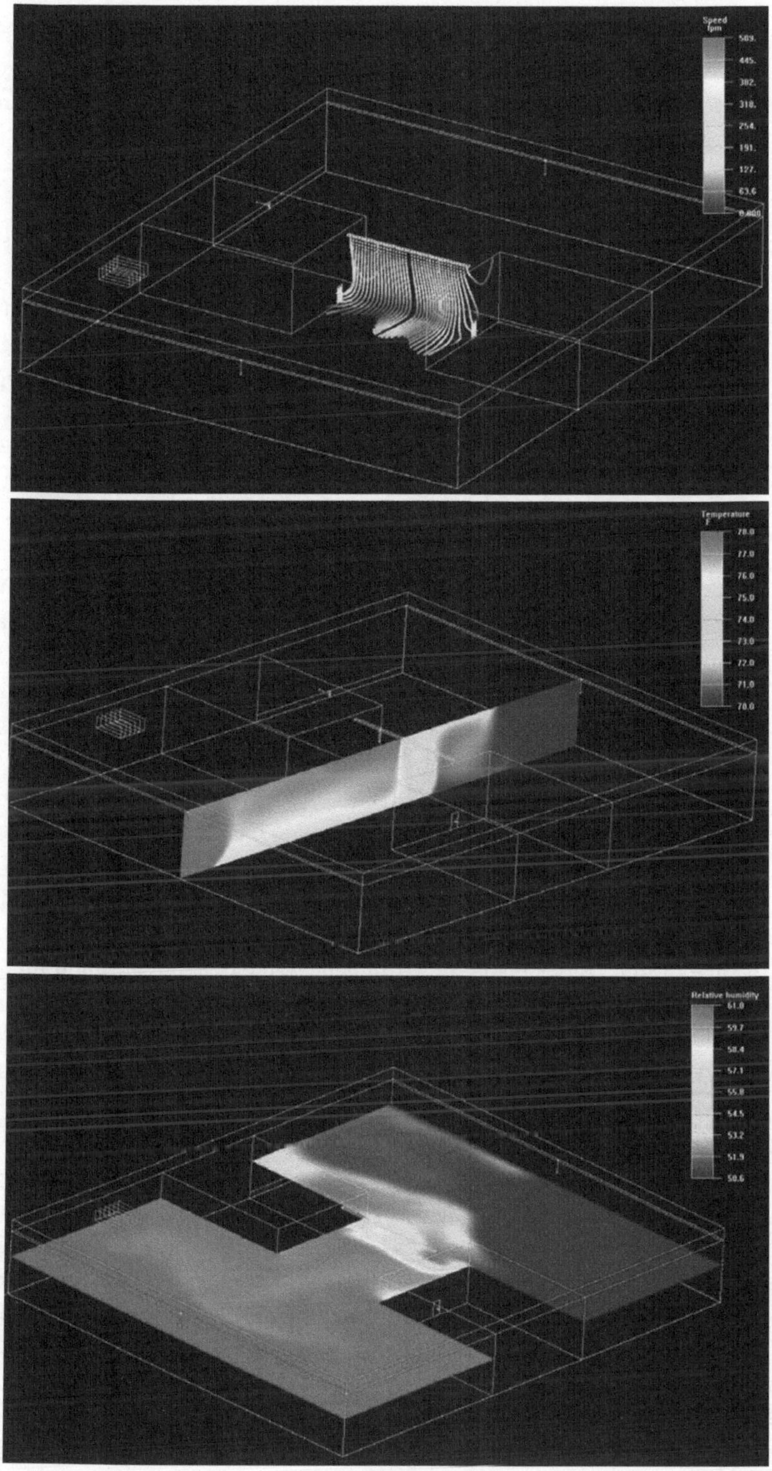

Figure 20 Wexner Center for the Arts environmental simulations, depicting a proposed air curtain and the resulting distribution of temperature and relative humidity in gallery spaces.

the Wexner Center as a manifesto against traditional museum typologies.[201] Inadvertently, Eisenman's conceptual attack subjected the artwork to collateral physical damage. The galleries could not maintain a constant temperature. A lack of sufficient thermal breaks in the museum's aluminum-frame facade led to 40-degree temperature fluctuations. There were areas of condensation and leaks in the roof. The intensity of natural light in the building was overwhelming. Curators could not live with the original building as an environment for putting sensitive artifacts on display.

Arup was originally commissioned by the Wexner administration just to evaluate the work of another engineering firm, and only later to suggest its own changes to the performance of the building.[202] The Arup team accepted the project with the goal "to not compromise Eisenman's design."[203] At the time of the museum's construction, geometric descriptions of the Wexner Center were unmanageable. In geometric terms, the Wexner Center was too ambitious. The building systems and analysis tools of the time could not support the geometry, which included both rectilinear and cylindrical volumes intersecting at odd angles and irregular intervals. Computational fluid dynamics techniques for assessing the interior environment were not widely available. Without sophisticated simulation tools, the original engineers only knew how to follow best practices. However, Eisenman's form didn't follow any established practices. The Wexner Center was designed to challenge conventions of form, and it did, but not only in the way that its architect intended.

When Arup took on the renovation, their Facade Group was just starting to assemble the simulations necessary to handle the complex geometry from a performance perspective. The Wexner Center renovation was the first project in which they brought to bear different simulation types on the analysis of one facade.[204] Arup still had some problems with Eisenman's geometry, but its suite of simulations made the form manageable by representing it in a new performance-based way. Eisenman, who did not participate in the renovation, but gave his blessing to the project, accepted Arup's proposition that the intent of the Wexner Center's form and its performance could be separated as domains of work, but reintegrated to make a better building overall.

The Wexner Center example presents an extreme disconnection between the two meanings of form discussed earlier, as performance on the one hand, and intent on the other. This distinction echoes the long-standing philosophical debate described by Forty: is form a sensation or is it an idea?[205] As Forty explains, "one describes the property of things as they are known to the senses, the other as they are known to the mind."[206] Although it is troubling to separate sensations and ideas conceptually, this is a distinction that serves a strategic function in practice.

Arup engineers define their work on the Wexner Center in terms of this pragmatic distinction. The idea behind the form was highly prized by the museum administration. However, the form as it could be known by the senses – in terms of temperature, humidity, and light – was problematic and should be fixed. Eisenman accepted this distinction as a professional one. In 2005, he was interviewed about the project by the *New York Times* and explained therein that performance problems are not his concern as an architect. "That's not what we do well."[207]

On the Sydney Opera House, there was a compromise between Arup and Utzon. The collaborators had to change the geometry of the Opera House roofs significantly in order to suit the constraints of structural performance testing. Intent and performance converged. On the Wexner Center, Arup was able to preserve the intent, by maintaining the geometry, and still make changes to the performance of the building – how it felt inside. The space of alternatives for the museum was defined originally by Eisenman's geometry, considered to be the intent of the building, and only later extended to account for building performance, made visible through Arup's suite of computer simulations.

Repeat Performances

The amount of unmediated natural light in the Wexner Center was among the building's primary difficulties. In museums, lighting conditions are often strictly regulated by curators. Natural light sources are important for displaying artwork under full spectrum, but direct natural light can also be harmful to sensitive materials or cause excessive glare for visitors. Thus, the space of natural lighting alternatives in museums is narrowly defined. Lighting designers, a broad professional group that might include individuals trained in engineering or theater, work with a range of simulations to define the shared space in which aesthetic and technical constraints can be satisfied. Recent projects from the Arup Lighting Group illustrate how the latest computer simulations satisfy strictly defined performances in buildings. Numerical and visual simulations can help lighting designers and their clients converge on a "satisficing" design solution.

The light levels in the Wexner Center defied standard, numerically-defined rules of illuminating art. Numerical goals are not the only representations brought by lighting designers to the service of predicting interior conditions: calculations, computer models, paper models, scale models, and full-scale mock-ups are all used in conjunction. However, the strictly numerical foot-candle value remains a powerful means of describing and regulating light.[208] One of the established references for setting light levels in museums is *The Museum Environment* by Garry Thomson, first published in 1978.[209] Arup lighting designers still call it their bible. Their recommendations for the renovation of the Wexner Center define good lighting performance in the numerical terms of Thomson's book.

However, even when the Arup Lighting Group begins its work early on in a project, during the conceptual design phase, severe constraints still shape their work. The group's incorporation of numerical standards for light levels in museums has led to a kind of aesthetic convergence. Take, as an example, the roof of the Nasher Sculpture Center in Dallas, Texas, designed in collaboration with the architecture office of Renzo Piano. The roof is composed of a field of tiny, identical cast-aluminum apertures. The torqued, cylindrical shape of each opening creates a limiting condition that keeps out the direct rays of the severe Texas sun, while creating a diffuse, even quality of light inside the galleries.

The Nasher Sculpture Center roof is the result of a simulation process aimed at optimizing and homogenizing illuminance levels on the artwork. Oscar Davis, a senior lighting consultant, explains how on many recent museum projects, Arup has worked with architects to develop fenestration and shading systems to block all direct natural light and UV rays.[210] These systems are designed to allow only indirect, filtered illumination to reach the artwork. "What gets inside remains constant," says Davis. For the Nasher Center, the design process revolved around the numerical goal of preserving stable illuminance levels and creating consistent perceptual experiences for visitors.

However, even the Nasher Center's optimized roof does not provide total consistency. Natural-source light levels change over the course of each day and throughout the year. Lighting designers found they could further develop

Figure 21
Nasher Sculpture Center roof from above.

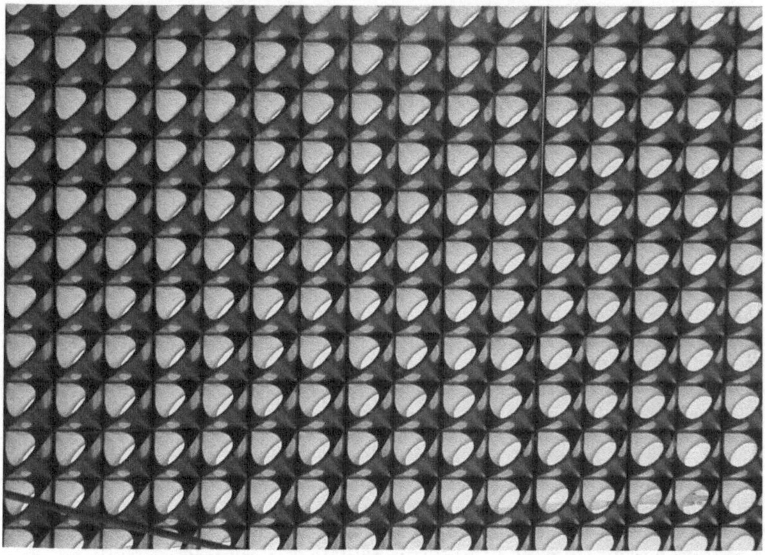

Figure 22
Nasher Sculpture Center roof from below.

their approach to creating consistent visual environments through a combination of computer simulation and automation. On the North Carolina Museum of Art in Raleigh, designed with the architects Thomas Phifer and Partners, artificial and natural light are blended through a translucent dropped ceiling in order to achieve a consistency all day and all year long. For museum curators, consistency means flexibility. Oscar Davis describes light levels as optimal throughout the Raleigh space. When light levels are constant throughout a museum, curators can place artwork almost anywhere. Through their use of numerically-oriented lighting simulations, lighting designers work toward a set of homogeneous museum spaces across time and geography.

These museums embody the idea of the "white cube," a prototypically modern space for display. Aesthetically, these spaces are the inverse of the Wexner Center: neutral realms for curating anything, anywhere. The Nasher Sculpture Center and the North Carolina Museum of Art were designed with attention to numerically defined performance. As in the case of early modern acoustics, the aesthetics of light have converged around a singular objective.[211] In acoustical design, that objective was an optimal, low reverberation time; in lighting design, the goal has been to achieve just the right illuminance level. However, these numerically-oriented simulations create a narrow space in which to evaluate the quality of light in museums. Architect William Porter warns that we may be losing "the vocabulary necessary to deal with a diverse range of lighting conditions."[212]

More recently, museum projects at Arup are moving beyond the goal of optimization and reliance on quantitative values. For the Caixa Forum in

Madrid, a former power station converted into a museum by the architects Herzog and de Meuron, the Arup Lighting Group aims to bring a range of natural light conditions into galleries, creating transient, heterogeneous spaces for display. Designers used visualization, instead of simply calculation, to test a variety of combined natural and artificial light conditions and created a tailored look for each space. As a result, artwork in the Caixa Forum must be arranged with consideration for the dynamic conditions of light in the building. The project represents a break from Arup's controlled approach to lighting in museums and its reliance on numerically-oriented solutions. Computer simulations still play a role in the shaping of the visually dynamic spaces of the Caixa Forum. However, these simulations, used to shape variability as easily as consistency, are being co-opted for an alternative aesthetics of light.

On the Caixa Forum project, visualizations or visual light simulations opened a range of new discussions about the sensation of form, or "what light is doing."[213] This new space of alternatives brings together quantitative and qualitative ways of evaluating form. Radiance, a ray-tracing software system, is currently the predominant simulator in use within the Arup Lighting Group. Radiance is a collection of tools in UNIX, "almost a way of thinking, more than a single piece of software," explains Michael Cullen, a British lighting designer. It was quickly accepted within Arup because of its ability to deliver photorealistic renderings and the opportunity to preview visual experiences. Although Radiance can also generate predictions of performance in terms of illuminance values, the simulation's images are of interest because they have enabled a new exchange among lighting designers, their clients, and their collaborators. Initially, explains Cullen, architects were nervous about accepting visualizations, especially at early phases of the design process. For Cullen's lighting group, it was the Mercedes-Benz Design Center in Sindelfingen, Germany, designed between 1993 and 1998, that "put lighting on the map" at Arup.[214] Within the context of that project, lighting became accepted both as a technical practice involving computer simulations and as a perspective on the performance of form.

Renzo Piano was hired by Mercedes as the architect for its Design Center, where car designers routinely use the reflections of parallel, tubular lights placed overhead to analyze the complex curves of vehicles in design. By examining the way reflections are distorted on the curved metal surfaces, car designers can determine the implications for manufacturing such surfaces on a mass scale. One of Mercedes' directives was that the Design Center must have studios where car designers can build full-size models of their designs. This directive came with a formal constraint: spaces designed for such modeling work should have only artificially controlled lighting, no natural light. Renzo Piano's architects challenged the assumption that natural light would interfere with car modeling. His architects searched for a way to bring daylight into the Mercedes studio spaces without disturbing the ability of car designers to conduct their curvature analysis. In other words, the architects wanted to change the intent of the design space, by opening it to the outside, without compromising its visual performance. The car designers at Mercedes were apprehensive.

Arup suggested the use of their new photorealistic visualization techniques in order to evaluate how daylight might interfere with curvature analysis. In order to convince Piano's architects and Mercedes administrators and designers, Arup introduced Radiance. Arup lighting designers met with Piano to discuss the lighting approach, then carried out their analysis on several alternate schemes. Their computers took five full days of rendering time to produce each variation.[215]

Figure 23
Mercedes-Benz Design Center in Sindelfingen: light simulation variations.

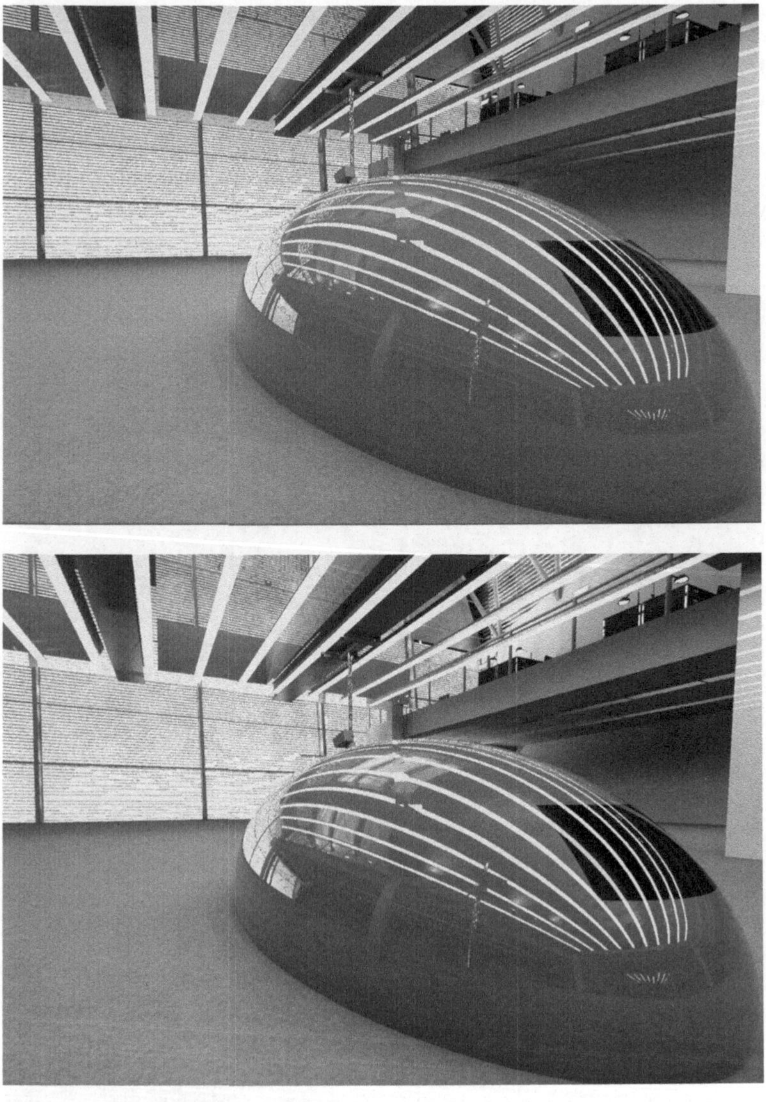

Figure 23
Continued.

The resulting images shaped a new space of evaluation for the design participants. By using the photorealistic visualization techniques of Radiance, Arup lighting designers were able to convince clients that daylight from the windows proposed by Piano would not interfere with reading reflections. In this way, the form of the Mercedes-Benz Design Center was resolved through the simulation of visibility in the room. Radiance shaped a new space of shared experience, in which Piano's radical intent for redesigning the Mercedes studios could be reconciled with the client's need for a consistent visual environment.[216]

As an aside, Cullen explains that it was the personal relationship between Renzo Piano and Franklin Mapes, the project leader at Arup, that enabled Radiance's simulated images to function as a medium of exchange. Piano trusted Mapes to provide a valid demonstration of the lighting in the space because Mapes knew how to create a simulation that would satisfy Piano's personal needs. For instance, Piano hated looking at the screen, so Mapes spent the money necessary to print out each rendering on paper. For Piano, it was important to be able to hold the renderings and interact with them. "You have to take into account the idiosyncrasies of people," explains Cullen. As I have shown, simulations must be tailored for a particular audience, even down to the mode of presentation. In the case of the Mercedes-Benz Design Center, Arup was able to negotiate a role for itself in the evaluation of form because its visualizations met the expectations of both collaborators and clients. The space of alternatives is inevitably a social space.

Performance by Intent

Computer simulations can help designers to isolate the performance of form from its intent. However, articulating form as a performance is much more than a technical task. Performance is socially established. Designers must build consensus around the parameters of experience and the goals of good form. The Arup SoundLab is one of the most convincing virtual reality machines that Arup possesses today; it has been written about widely in professional journals and popular publications. Francis Martin, of the Arup Acoustics Group in New York City, explains that acoustical simulations or "auralizations" produced in the Arup SoundLab allow form to be explored as an acoustical sensation. For Martin, immersive simulations make ideas into experiences. Through computer simulations, "people are rediscovering things about the architecture that made the room sound the way it sounded."[217] They enable acoustical experiences of the past and present to be exposed, analyzed, compared, and tinkered with.

Historian Emily Thompson has written about acoustical simulation as a post-modern soundscape, in which "the past – be it gothic, baroque, or modern – [is] like an endlessly stimulating old album of phonograph recordings from which we are privileged to pick and choose."[218] Architects and clients can select from among a history of acoustical experiences or simply tinker with alternatives. Martin explains, "If you can get the spacings right, suddenly the room sounds huge and expansive and wide. The Arup SoundLab allows us to play with dimensions to see how they fundamentally affect the way that we hear."

Martin was trained as a musician and a scientist, but he is working toward an identity as a designer. Professing an understanding of form in terms of acoustical performance has enabled Martin and his colleagues to establish powerful creative roles among both architects and clients. Martin's Acoustics

Group has created a place for itself within the conceptual, form-finding phases of many design projects by leveraging the use of the Arup SoundLab. Linus Russell, who works with Martin, explains how the simulator enabled his team to claim a place for themselves as part of the acoustical renovation of the Lincoln Center's Alice Tully Hall, one of the most well-known, if not well-regarded, concert halls in New York City.

Jaffe Holden, an acoustical consultant in the northeastern United States, was originally selected to design a new acoustical experience as part of the first major renovation of Alice Tully Hall since its opening in 1969. Arup was hired separately, as a consultant to the architects of the renovation, Diller, Scofidio, and Renfro, to address structural and mechanical issues. Using a suite of acoustical models and simulations, including the Arup SoundLab, Russell and his associates challenged the exclusive authority of Jaffe Holden. Arup's technological tools gave them authority as peer reviewers in the acoustical design process.[219] "[Jaffe Holden's] tools are not as sophisticated," explains Russell.[220] "The clients wanted to be here. They trusted us. [Jaffe Holden] doesn't have a sound lab like this one." Over the course of the Alice Tully Hall renovation, the Arup SoundLab became a primary space for design decision-making. The success of the Arup SoundLab is part of a culture at Arup of using simulation to bring designs into the virtual realm as a means of gaining greater control over their form.

In Martin's group, form is articulated as an acoustic experience that can be identified, evaluated, replicated, and controlled. The group enables this transformation through a range of techniques, including the prominent use of the Arup SoundLab. Although Arup acousticians originally intended to use the device for themselves, "so that we can listen to our designs," it eventually became popular with clients, professional performers, and architects. Now it serves as a primary setting for discussions on acoustics among diverse design participants:

> The thing about the Soundlab is that you've got everybody in the same room at the same time. They all hear exactly the same thing. You have the discussion in the room. You make the design decisions then you move on, so it's a much more collaborative process.[221]

The Arup SoundLab is both a physical and a conceptual space in which participants in design can come to a consensus on what constitutes a good form from an acoustic perspective. Physically, it is a small room, approximately a cube, with interior dimensions of about 12 feet x 12 feet x 12 feet and 12 speakers arranged spherically on the surrounding walls and ceiling. Conceptually, it enables acoustic experience to define a shared space of alternatives.

The system relies on the principle of auralization to create an aural rendering of a space. Renderings start with an impulse, or "click," first emitted in a real space or in the computational space of a geometric model. The resulting reverberations are measured and used to create an acoustical signature for that room. Another sound – usually a piece of music – is then recorded in an anechoic chamber, a room that absorbs all sound and effectively has a reverberation time of zero. "In a good anechoic chamber," says Russell, "you can hear the blood pumping in your veins." The perfect chamber would be so unnatural that it would make you sick just to be there.

The recorded music is then augmented through a process called "convolution." The resulting music is what you hear in the Arup SoundLab, a simulation of what the anechoic performance might sound like in the real hall or geometric model that you started out with. Russell calls this a "spatialization" or the "rendering of space." As with the visualizations created by Cullen, sensation replaces calculation as a means of evaluating form.

In one of my tours of the Arup SoundLab, I sit amid a class of undergraduate architects from the City College of New York, led by Sarah Solis, an architect who works at Arup and teaches part-time. Solis's students have come to Arup's office for an experience of professional practice. Jacob Lutz, a recent hire at Arup, has been tasked with giving a simple demonstration of the Arup SoundLab. On a projection screen in front of us, Lutz presents two virtual models. He calls these "boxes," not concert halls or buildings. On one side of the display, he shows us a "narrow box." This box has a reverberation time of 2.0 seconds. On the other side of the display is a "wide box" with the same reverberation time, also 2.0 seconds. The fledgling acoustician puts Handel's "Water Music" on the Arup SoundLab speakers as it would be heard, first in the narrow box, then in the wide box. Following the demonstration, he asks for our impressions. "What do you hear?" "What do you like?" At first, we are silent. We lack the vocabulary to classify our experience or express our impressions. How do you talk about an acoustic experience without a shared vocabulary?

For an experience to be identified, it needs a discourse, a shared means of expression. Discrete acoustic experiences and their attributes must be identifiable in a common way. One reoccurring problem is that acousticians and architects have different meanings for words like "tone," "clarity," and "intimacy." These are multivalent terms. For example, architectural intimacy might have to do with the physical proximity between the musician and the audience. Meanwhile, acoustic intimacy may concern the reverberation time that the audience experiences. If the audience is close to a reflective surface, they can experience acoustic intimacy; it will sound as if they are close to the musicians, even if they are physically far away. So at the back of a concert hall, it is possible to have acoustic, but not architectural, intimacy. The demonstration we are getting is meant to develop a shared discourse. Lutz and Martin explain it this way:

> The interesting thing about it is that you have to develop a common language. What we mean by certain words: direct sound, reflections, reverberance, envelopment, proximity, intimacy. All of those words mean different things to different people. So the first part of the conversation is always the basic demonstration that you had, to get some commonality and some understanding in the words that you are using, so that they understand what we mean, then use that in discussion.[222]

In contrast, another acoustician, Russell, claims that the room "does away with linguistic vocabulary." But linguistic vocabulary, what I have been calling discourse, does not go away in the Arup SoundLab; it spreads in a very short period of time. So why does Russell say that the room does away with linguistic vocabulary? Perhaps he means that the vocabulary appears transparent. In the Arup SoundLab, vocabulary is used as a pointer to shared experience. In this setting, vocabulary may appear transparent, because we can make a seemingly effortless link between words and shared virtual experiences.

However, the apparent transparency of vocabulary in the Arup SoundLab is part of its power. Michael Reddy, an early researcher in the field of cognitive science, has demonstrated that, given a vocabulary, we must each construct our own meanings from a repertoire of experiences.[223] Thus, meaningful communication is built on common experiences. The Arup SoundLab demonstrates this by enabling both new kinds of shared events and improved conversations, but we should be wary of believing that such simulations can deliver one objective experience to all participants. That notion would be contrary to venerable psychological and architectural conceptions of experience that define it as categorically personal.[224] Experience is not something external that happens to us; it is something each of us must construct.

The Arup SoundLab helps participants converge toward a common discourse so they can collectively identify distinct experiences and their salient characteristics. Experiences can thus be compared. The ability to perform this kind of shared comparison is the pay-off of the Arup SoundLab. The result is a more controlled conversation:

> The discussion is always a very healthy flow when you are in that room, because everybody's heard the same thing . . . you've got eight options on the screen . . . then they listen to the subtleties and work out the answer and it's done in two hours.[225]

Furthermore, the apparent manipulability of experiences in the Arup SoundLab recalls one of the differences I have explained, between computer simulation and other static rationalizations, such as perspective.[226] Computer simulations differ in their ability to respond dynamically to user interaction; they appear to give you control over the parameters of experience. Back in the Arup SoundLab, Lutz demonstrates how variations in the design of a subway station can be compared, evaluated, and augmented.

The central acoustical problem of subway stations is that they are too reverberant. An announcement on the loudspeaker is engulfed in reverberance after the first couple of words. Beyond that, you usually cannot understand anything else that is said. Lutz pulls up a prepared simulation ofthe public announcement system for the Second Avenue Subway Project in New York City. He constructs the experience of the impaired public announcement system by layering sounds in the following sequence:

1 Voice Alone
2 Voice + Microphone
3 Voice + Microphone + Booth Noise
4 Voice + Microphone + Booth Noise + Speaker
5 Voice + Microphone + Booth Noise + Speaker + 4.0 Second Reverberation Time of the Station and Station Noise.

With each layer, the sound gets worse and more distorted. By the final layer, the voice is almost totally drowned out and unintelligible. Then he demonstrates the fix, by working backward:

1 Isolate the Booth and the Cable.
2 Improve the Microphone.
3 Improve the Speaker System.
4 Improve the Reverberation Time.

By defining an external, replicable acoustic experience and taking it apart, one component at a time, Lutz reconstructs the problem of the Second Avenue subway terminal. This demonstration creates an intimate connection between words and signals, between talking about designs and experiencing them in the Arup SoundLab.

Conceptions of structure, environment, light, and sound have shifted along with the simulation technologies of the last few decades. Emily Thompson explains this well for the case of acoustics:

> Acoustical technology in the modern era had been dedicated to eliminating the effect of space and replacing it with one best sound, the modern sound. Postmodern acoustical technologies, in contrast, summon forth the sound of space so easily and in so many varieties, we hardly know what to listen to first.[227]

Arup acousticians have capitalized on post-modern conceptions of sound. They have turned the exploration of varied acoustic experience into a competitive niche in architecture. Martin articulates how the Arup SoundLab is used to control the value of design through the identification of architecture with controllable experience:[228]

> Every single aspect, if you start thinking about how the outside noise relationship relates to the inside noise relationship, how the design of this partition relates to how much sound goes from room to room, what the acoustics of this room are like. Every element of that can be broken down, can be explained, can be subjectively value engineered. The term value engineering is a misnomer because people will try to reduce the cost of something, but that often means putting a value on whether something is necessary or not necessary in a design.[229]

Arup is putting a value on form in a variety of domains, not just those covered in this chapter. However, simulations like the Arup SoundLab contribute to the production of contemporary conceptions of form in complex ways that transcend cost value. Defining good form in architecture is a strategic compromise between computer simulation and other personal and disciplinary ways of knowing. By working toward a pluralistic formalism, we can acknowledge these dynamics and encourage the development of more inclusive shared spaces for design in architecture. I believe this can lead to more nuanced and multivalent formal results.

Pluralists at Play

Many designers and researchers have called for a pluralist approach to architecture. One example that can enrich my discussion here is the work of John Habraken on "Concept Design Games."[230] In the 1980s, Habraken, then a professor in the Department of Architecture at MIT, developed a research method to study design from a pluralist perspective. Together with a post-doctoral researcher, Mark Gross, and a group of architecture students, Habraken examined design work through the vehicle of play. Their play was structured around the development and use of games as tools for constructing and testing theories of design. Habraken wrote at length about the similarities between design and gaming:

> When designing involves the interaction of many actors, all involved with transforming an artifact, we see similarities with board games . . . As when designing, players must fit pieces into an existing field; rules, conventions, and principles limit how they may

move; and they make flexible, negotiable arrangements about what conventions and rules to use in a given situation.[231]

Consider two basic assumptions that Habraken's games make about design. First, that design is a social activity, necessitating cooperation and negotiation among many actors. Second, that design is a process of morphological change; designs evolve over time. As simplified arenas for collective form-making, Concept Design Games clarify the anatomy of shared spaces of alternatives, highlighting the way that designers interact with each other and the dynamic context in which they work.

In order to emulate various interactions and contexts for design, each Concept Design Game has its own materials and rules.[232] In one example, called simply "The Silent Game," players take turns manipulating abstract forms without speaking. The Silent Game can be played in many different ways.[233] In all of its variants, the game asks: can form speak for us? What can it say? This game in particular raises questions about the autonomy of form and the necessity of interpretation, which can come from different, conflicting perspectives. Unlike design practice, each Concept Design Game makes its own space of alternatives explicit; it is readily visible in the pieces, the game board, and the rules of play.

Unfortunately, Habraken and Gross considered the results of their game play to be inconclusive. As I have illustrated throughout this book, design cannot easily be abstracted from its social and technological context. However, Habraken discovered that trying to do so can be quite revealing. In fact, he found that developing new games is more useful than playing them.[234] In order to make a new Concept Design Game, one must grapple with abstracting the complexity of design practice. Developing a Concept Design Game forces one to ask, what is design? How can the activity be distilled without losing what is fundamental?

These questions echo the ones routinely posed by architects and engineers as they consider the implications of developing or adopting new software: can human activities be abstracted by technology? How will design change along with its social and technological context? What should be preserved in design, if anything? I believe, along with Habraken, that a pluralistic perspective can help us think about these questions by acknowledging various answers as equally valid.[235] Within each architectural project, many concerns must be reconciled but not conflated. In design, as in Habraken's games, the shared space of alternatives is the place where participants agree on a good form, even if for their own purposes.

I do not want directly to equate computer simulations and games. When designers build computer simulations or put them into practice, they do not leave aside their professional objectives; they are not simply out to win. In fact, as I have shown again and again, designers are particularly sensitive to how computer simulations fit into broader systems of identity formation, knowledge creation, and form-making. Only the most extreme technology enthusiasts claim that computer simulations can emulate all aspects of design.

Habraken's work is useful for thinking about computer simulations, not because his games are simulations themselves or vice versa. Concept Design Games help us understand the pluralisms within the design process, illuminating the context in which computer simulations are put into play.

Chapter 6

Designers in Dialog

Narratives: Past and Present

Learning about architecture usually means looking at buildings. But if we want to understand cultures of architecture, we should listen as well.[236] Indeed, one method of describing a culture is by accounting for the narrative models that it offers for interpreting environments and events.[237] In this sense, personal accounts of lived experiences reflect broader patterns and norms. I track changing professional narratives in order to understand the evolution of cultures in architecture. For example, we can recall the voices from Arup's 1963 symposium (see Chapter 1) and ask, how have the hopes and anxieties of designers changed in the intervening 50 years?

At the time of the symposium, members of Arup wondered what computers would take off their hands: tedious routines or critical judgments? Over the past 50 years, designers have negotiated control with, and through, their computers. For some, computing has become a means of relinquishing responsibility, in order to achieve new levels of complexity, out of reach by manual techniques. For others, computing is a way of keeping one's hand in design, either virtually, through the development of new software, or by redefining creativity as an attribute of a computer operator. Designers are making these trade-offs strategically. Working in architecture today, in 2012, means redefining your roles and relationships to increase control and connectivity, even if it sometimes comes at the expense of a deeper intimacy with other people or materials.

Participants of the symposium agreed that computers would necessitate new roles in architecture and engineering. As predicted, "special" people have arrived in architecture. However, these new practitioners did not originate outside of the field, nor are they simply mediators for the machine. Designers – architects, acousticians, structural engineers, fire safety engineers, and others – are reinventing themselves as the "special" men and women who will define architecture in the context of computer simulations.

Participants wondered whether the new machines would change the way designers think. Would computers make designers more systematic? Algorithms, the logical representations that run on computers, are explicit for those who program them. However, algorithms are low-level descriptions of design. They cannot be said to encode design thinking or systematize it. Furthermore, most uses of computing in architecture do not involve programming. Those who use computer software developed by others are not exposed to the underlying algorithms. These designers are content to work on the surface of software; they have adopted a post-modern sensibility about computing. Computers are transparent in a post-modern sense; that is, not when their underlying workings are revealed, but when they just work. This surface transparency means that computers operate systematically so people do not have to.

Finally, participants also speculated that computing might give rise to more complex designs. Today, computers are enabling more sophisticated descriptions of designs.[238] Sometimes, these elaborate representations enable designs that were previously unimaginable, or untestable. However, I have shown that better simulations can also simply enable more precise consistency and homogeneity.

The Limits of Narrative

The stories I have told about how professionals in architecture have dealt with computing over the past 50 years are part of a broader, evolving set of narratives about what design means in cultures of computer simulation. They illustrate how simulations shape the climate in which designers work out projects as well as loftier conceptions of professional identity, disciplinary knowledge, and good form.

However, narrative is a narrow window into the complex interactions that constitute practice. Narratives are partial, transient, and shaped for particular audiences. When we rely on narrative alone to understand social dynamics, we miss more fine-grained activities. Unconscious practices, unacknowledged workarounds, and unseen gestures conceal important aspects of design. Other avenues of study, like consistent close observation, can reveal some of these.[239] However, the incompleteness of narratives tells us much about the situated roles of designers.[240] Narratives reflect the professional positions from which they are constructed. We can take conflicting or unstable narratives as evidence of cultural disputes and professional shifts, large and small. For example, when designers disagree about who should be at the center of design – generalist architects, geometry specialists, or software developers – they are calling attention to important, but otherwise invisible, tensions in the distribution of design work. Moreover, the constructed on the fly nature of oral narrative histories presents an opportunity for researchers. A good interviewer works with a subject to develop nuanced, concrete accounts of events and resonant interpretations. Even when activities are observed directly, narratives are necessary to make sense of interactions and artifacts.[241] Geertz writes that all narratives are fictions, in the sense that they are made.[242] But much like simulations themselves, narratives are useful fictions and indispensable explanations. We need narratives to understand the significance of events for their participants; there are few other ways of revealing the webs of meaning that people weave.

In this chapter, I examine the structure of contemporary narrative webs in architecture to uncover new patterns of human–machine–environment interaction. My examination begins with a consideration of the professional narratives put forward in this book. How can these narratives be characterized? What are the implications of recent changes? Are some narratives better than others? In order to answer this last question, I take as an example the use of an implicit metaphor in many of the accounts in this book, that simulation is theater. By probing this metaphor, we can understand the practice of simulation more deeply. The production of building performance, the design of analytical scenarios, and the representation of human experience in buildings, all done through simulation, are a balance between immersive and critical ways of engaging audiences. Creating a valid simulation is like creating a successful theatrical performance; it is all about engaging your audience in the right way. We can distinguish between narratives that lead professionals toward more transparent, responsible relationships with audiences; and narratives that serve simply to maintain professional boundaries and obscure what designers do.

Narrative Models

"Stories happen to people who know how to tell them," writes the accomplished novelist Henry James.[243] This suggests that only those who know how to narrate simulations can produce them. Conversely, knowing how to produce a professional narrative in architecture increasingly means using the discourse of computer simulation. The interpretation of simulations cannot be disentangled from broader professional narratives, stories that designers tell to make sense of their work. Designers use *technical narratives* to explain how simulations function. They use *analytical narratives* to describe the problems that simulations address. They develop *methodological narratives* to explain the way they use simulations. Finally, they turn to *reflective narratives* to consider the effect of simulations on their professional roles. My work in this book can be summed up as a set of *cultural narratives* on simulations. Drawing upon present relationships with people, machines, and environments, my subjects and I develop narratives and weigh them against one another as a way of thinking through what architecture means in a rapidly changing socio-technical context.

At Arup, designers are already beginning to see how narratives structure their work. "We are moving away from structured databases and towards stories. There is an acknowledgement that people like to work with stories," says Alvin Bernard, who works on issues of knowledge management. He explains that "simulations, to an extent, build upon stories that people already know about how buildings work and how design works." Therefore, narrative is the very structure through which designers explain simulations to themselves, regulators, collaborators, and clients.

I believe, along with psychologist Jerome Bruner, that the study of thought processes has much to gain from fields that take narrative itself as their subject. When Bruner examines autobiographical narratives for psychological inroads to understanding self-perception, he turns to an early twentieth-century group of literary critics, the Russian Formalists, for help.[244] The Russians break down narratives into three parts. Bruner translates these as theme, discourse, and genre. My breaking down of professional narratives in architecture follows the tripartite structure of Bruner's adopted formalism quite closely. First, I am interested in a series of themes that professional narratives invariably deal with; I call these identity, knowledge, and form. Second, the terms of discourse that are used in professional narratives are an important part of my study. Discourses, the interpretive languages of designers, shape their shared spaces of alternatives. Third, I pay attention to the genres used in professional narratives. In my work, these genres are best understood as layers of interpretation: technical, analytical, methodological, reflective, cultural. With new technologies for computer simulation, discourses have changed more than themes or genres.

Although Bruner's themes are meant to be timeless, I will not claim that my themes endure outside of twentieth- or twenty-first century architecture. The themes of identity, knowledge, and form, often invoked in contemporary professional narratives, have structured this book. Narratives on identity, described in Chapter 3, "'Special' Men and Universal Machines," express the roles and relationships that are available for designers. Narratives on knowledge, explored in Chapter 4, "How do Simulations Know?," articulate acceptable ways of developing, maintaining, and communicating beliefs among designers. Narratives on form, revealed in Chapter 5, "Towards a Pluralistic Formalism," define how designs are perceived and evaluated.

Meanwhile, discourses shape the shared spaces in which designers address the themes described above; they have changed noticeably with the evolution of computer simulations. The discourses around early efforts to apply computers to architecture were focused on the mechanical analysis of building performance: lighting designers spoke in terms of illuminance levels, acousticians assessed the reverberation time of sound, and fire safety engineers worried about structural failure. Using computer simulations, professionals are turning the focus from buildings to human experience. Today, in 2012, computer simulations are used in many areas of design to frame the performance of buildings in terms of human sensations and perceptual states: lighting designers now address visibility, acousticians discuss the experience of envelopment, and fire engineers fret about how people might escape from burning buildings. With this new attention on the human response to building performance, some designers are trying to reify a questionable conception of human experience: that it can be objectified, replicated, and controlled.[245]

Design narratives can also be categorized by genre. Each genre can be seen as a different layer of interpretation, addressing a distinct rhetorical function. At a technical level, design narratives are tools for quantification. At an analytical level, they are devices for problem solving. At a methodological level, they are plans for the organization of work. At a reflective level, they are instruments of self-analysis. At a cultural level, they define an epistemological community. These layers are deeply interrelated; one type of narrative builds upon another. Indeed, in this book I have made the point that new technical narratives developing around computer simulations affect the reflective narratives that designers use to think about their identities as professionals. Below I explain these levels in more detail and provide an example of each.

Technical narratives are stories about the mechanics of the design process. They might address the origins of simulation technologies, their underlying scientific models and data, or the interfaces through which designers encounter them. For example:

> Fablon works on the principle of dynamic relaxation, originally developed to perform non-linear analysis on the foundations for nuclear reactors. This technique uses an iterative approach to resolve the relationships among a number of independently defined elements. It has since been adopted as a technique for form-finding in cable and fabric structures. It would work for any non-linear structure.[246]

Analytical narratives are stories in which technologies for simulation are used to reason about particular design problems. These narratives are tailored for a specific audience; for instance, to argue for an optimal form or to bypass prescriptive regulations. Analytical narratives are sometimes referred to as "scenarios" by designers. It is through highly specific, numerically supported scenarios that inputs are assigned and outputs are evaluated for each simulation. For example:

> 9/11 was an unheard-of scenario. However, the day after 9/11, it was immediately in everyone's mind as a scenario. For instance, on the

> IFC2 building in Hong Kong, we were halfway to completion when 9/11 happened. The day after, the client wanted to know if it was going to be safe, would anyone want to occupy the upper storeys? News events are often the source of new scenarios. These are the events on clients' minds. When the suicide bombing happened in London, that became a scenario. Our security business has been very busy. Another current scenario is infection control in hospitals. This is a problem for airflow. This scenario is on the top of the agenda for the National Health Service.[247]

Methodological narratives explain how simulations fit into a broader design process. Unlike analytical narratives, methodological narratives are not about specific projects; they are explanations of how simulations are (or should be) applied. These stories are useful for understanding how simulations challenge the way designers organize their work and distribute design tasks among themselves. For example:

> Every single aspect, if you start thinking about how the outside noise relationship relates to the inside noise relationship, how the design of this partition relates to how much sound goes from room to room, what the acoustics of this room are like. Every element of that can be broken down, can be explained, can be subjectively value engineered. The term value engineering is a misnomer because people will try to reduce the cost of something, but that often means putting a value on whether something is necessary or not necessary in a design.[248]

Reflective narratives are stories in which designers reason about design as a domain of work. They may address the purposes of design, what makes a design good, or what it means to be a designer. Such narratives reveal how professionals see themselves and their work in the context of simulations. For example:

> Architects and engineers are at war. Engineers are perceived as the dumb guys. Architects are the artists. I couldn't understand this position. Now I am working almost as another architect. I focus on building rather than engineering or architecture. I tell the people that work with me that you have to learn the language of architecture. Talk in terms of texture and density, instead of torsion and shear. That way they don't think you are just another nerd.[249]

In my own writing, I use another recognizable narrative model: the cultural narrative. My cultural narratives account for the role of computer simulations in the construction of meaning in design. Cultural narratives are no truer than the other stories designers tell. The goal of my writing is to encourage a deeper discussion, one in which people inside and outside of architecture might think about how professional cultures are changing along with the technologies of simulation.

From Narrative to Theater

In professional narratives about computer simulations in architecture, designers often invoke discourses on performance, scenarios, audiences, and the dynamics of human experience. There is an implicit metaphor in these discussions that simulation is theater. With computer simulations, professional narratives take on qualities of theatricality. This metaphor offers more than a few useful terms for dealing with computer simulations. Taking seriously the metaphor that simulation is theater opens new questions, including: what kind of theater is it?[250]

The early twentieth-century German playwright and theorist Bertolt Brecht juxtaposes two types of theater: dramatic and dialogical (what he originally called epic theater).[251] This opposition can be helpful in understanding the different ways that designers use computer simulations to engage clients, collaborators, and regulators as audiences.

Brecht's work is motivated in part by dissatisfaction with the dramatic theater; he considers it a place of passivity for audiences. Brecht describes performance in the dramatic theater as an integrated experience enveloping the audience. He fears that the dramatic theater tries to universalize experience. It does not challenge audience members to examine the structure of the performance; it leaves them complacent.

In contrast, Brecht proposes the dialogical theater as a place of rational dialog among audiences and actors. The dialogical theater is an experience under construction, where the components of a performance are dissociated. Theorist David Krasner writes, "[Brecht] wanted spectators to reflect on the staged event, consider how it took shape in reality, and explore what can be done to change the course of events."[252]

Reflecting on the use of simulations in architecture, we can see connections to both the dramatic and the dialogical theaters. Using simulations in a dramatic fashion could mean that audiences – designers, clients, and regulators – understand architecture through the experience of simulation alone, a kind of virtual reality. Virtual experiences are produced through the manipulation of what Baudrillard has called "signs of the real" – visual, auditory, or other sensory cues forming the basis of a simulated reality.[253] Like the dramatic theater, virtual experiences present themselves as holistic. In dramatic or "total" theater, experience is constructed through the integration of music, text, and visual arts.

The German opera composer Richard Wagner called this integration of the arts *Gesamtkunstwerk*, the same German term that was used by Gropius to describe total architecture.[254] It is interesting to consider that the concept of total architecture, first written about by Gropius, and later embraced by Arup, probably had its roots in the same cultural history as the dramatic theater. Today, in 2012, the pursuit of total architecture at Arup has evolved into an interest in integrating simulations. In this sense, the immersive software environment, Realtime, can be considered an example of a dramatic simulation, combining performances from many specialized domains: acoustics, lighting, airflow, and structures.

In contrast, the dialogical theater establishes a critical distance between the components of performance; music, text, and visual arts are dissociated. Brecht's dialogical plays present the theater as an experience under construction. Similarly, computer simulations are sometimes presented as under construction. Talcott Saunders notes that it is sometimes healthy to present aspects of design as distinct and in conflict through the use of simulation.[255] From Saunders' point of view, integration should occur through discussion and reflection on the various components of design. For critical and dialogical purposes, integration is problematic, masking the integrity and structure of individual simulations. Analysis often works best when it is used to isolate and examine a particular phenomenon like airflow, acoustics, structures, or lighting. Integrated simulations are dramatic. They can create a holistic experience for audiences, but that experience is inscrutable.

Furthermore, Brecht writes that the audience should be distanced from the performance. He called this the *Verfremdungseffekt*, an estrangement or alienation meant to induce critical thought. Brecht wants audiences to approach theater rationally, rather than through uncritical experience. Audiences of the dialogical theater are made aware of the "fourth wall" of the stage, the invisible barrier that, in the dramatic theater, separates actors from audiences.[256] The result, writes Brecht, is that rather than rendering the audience complacent, the dialogical theater "arouses the capacity for action."[257]

Applying Brecht's dialogical model in the context of this book suggests that computer simulation can become a "What if?" game in which the audience is implicated in the making of decisions. This approach is already evident in the way some designers talk about the responsibility of computer simulation. Patrick McCormack at Oasys argues that good simulations, their graphics, interfaces, and manipulability, encourage more interrogation of what is behind the software.

The metaphor that simulation is theater can also reveal something about the construction of professional identities in architecture. The identity of characters in the dramatic theater is unproblematic: the actor is the character. In the dialogical theater, actors reflect critically on their roles, even while they play them out. They may even go so far as to comment on their characters in the third person. Brecht writes, "The actors, too, refrained from going over wholly into their role, remaining detached from the character they were playing and clearly inviting criticism of him."[258] In order to have an open, dialogical use of computer simulation in architecture, practitioners need to reflect critically on their roles and relationships. Opening professional identities to explicit discussion and negotiation can illuminate the conflicting perspectives on simulation.

Most uses of computer simulation have both dramatic and dialogical aspects. Practitioners challenge audiences to approach designs emotionally as well as rationally. The production of building performance through computer simulations can be a balance between immersive and critical ways of engaging with audiences. The metaphor of the theater reveals the importance of audiences in the practice of simulation. Creating a valid simulation, like creating a successful theatrical performance, requires connecting with your audience in the right way.

In simulations that are both immersive and distancing, different dimensions of design are juxtaposed. For example, in the simulations of Stansted Airport (see Figure 12), Arup presented regulators with knowledge through the immersive experience of their graphics, but also through discussion and critical reflection about the underlying evidence and algorithms. In the example of the Wexner Center for the Arts (see Chapter 5), Arup issued a report to the administration of the museum that described form as both an integrated performance and as a set of dissociated components. By showing both the dramatic and the dialogical perspectives on the Wexner Center, Arup illustrated how performance would be improved by changing some of the components of the museum, such as its facade and mechanical systems. In the design of concert halls like Alice Tully Hall (see Chapter 5), Arup acousticians presented themselves as playing multiple roles, or taking on a dynamic identity. They are both scientists and designers. They have a grasp on the technical underpinnings of the physics of sound, but they can also collaborate with designers on aesthetic decisions.

The Arup SoundLab most poignantly embodies this dual dynamic of the dramatic and the dialogical. It immerses audiences in acoustical experience and then lets them step back and look at how that experience is constructed; thus, both emotional and critical thinking are involved. Practitioners reach many audiences by presenting simulations that balance the dialogical and the dramatic. They use simulations to engage their audiences critically, but also to make them feel comfortable.

I want to acknowledge that the metaphor of the theater breaks down easily. We should not confuse simulation with theater. Audiences in the theater and in simulation differ greatly. Simulations allow design participants to circle around a performance and tinker with its premises. They open up shared spaces in which design participants can think and interact in new ways. In contrast to theater, the audiences of simulation are often more involved in establishing the premises upon which performances are based. In addition, the makers of simulations are routinely their own audiences; practitioners often make simulations for themselves. Although simulation is not theater, the metaphor affords new ways of discussing how new technologies might be used more productively by designers.

I should also note that for Brecht, the theater was more than mere entertainment or education. He saw the dramatic and dialogical theaters as social systems, supporting contradictory political agendas. Developing his theory of the theater during the 1930s in Germany, Brecht believed that the dramatic theater supported complacency among the public. It was the era of National Socialist Germany, and the dramatic work of Wagner produced a kind of nationalism that Brecht was wary of. Brecht's dialogical model was meant to combat over-exuberant nationalism by pushing the audience, particularly the proletariat, to think and to question their condition in society. In this sense, Brecht's dialogical theater was meant to be a catalyst not only for reflection, but for revolution.

Although I am not suggesting we see dramatic and dialogical uses of simulation in terms of nationalism, I do believe that simulation has a capacity to play a political role. For example, simulations that account for human experience in buildings take on the responsibility of representing the public and its needs. By representing people, simulations speak for them. In architecture, these simulations are used by practitioners to challenge established building regulations and the politics that underlie them. As long as practitioners continue to use simulations to represent the public and scrutinize or overturn regulations, they have an imperative to adopt a broader discourse about politics; conversely, politicians have an imperative to engage more actively in design discourse.

In *Science in Action*, Bruno Latour explains how to take apart scientific and technological black boxes like computer simulations for political purposes.[259] He encourages us to engage "science in-the-making," as opposed to "science ready-made."[260] Similarly, engaging simulations in architecture, not just dramatically but also as dialogical performances, as architecture in-the-making, can encourage new critical narratives. By embracing and extending the metaphor of the theater, we can differentiate professional narratives based on their political implications: do they reassert traditional disciplinary boundaries or open up architecture to new forms of collective imagination? Simulating architecture in-the-making is the first step toward a new pluralism for designers.

Chapter 7

Human, Machine, and Environment

The narratives of designers in architecture are part of a much longer story about how today's computer simulations are reforming relationships in a range of human–machine–environment interactions.[261] As I have shown, such relationships are social; in a variety of ways, machines and environments represent their human authors. They embody the judgment, values, and histories of social groups. In this sense, interactions among people, machines, and environments are human conversations across time and space. I have explored one way of studying these conversations in this book, through the narratives of their participants. Future work might reveal alternative methods of seeing these interactions, which capture what narratives cannot. For now, I will close by reflecting on what narratives have shown in my stories of designers in the technological moment.

Professional Narratives

I have considered the implications of the shift to computer simulation and what it means for design practice in architecture. Designers, the broad range of creative practitioners who have a hand in design, are contemplating the new social and technological conditions for their work. They see existing conditions and imagine alternatives from new professional roles, embedded in rapidly changing networks of relationships. Acousticians, fire safety engineers, facade designers, and many others in the building industry are learning that the struggle for professional jurisdiction is increasingly a struggle for jurisdiction over computer simulations. Studying the socio-technical dynamics of their work helps us to understand all these participants as designers in their own way, exploring new forms of symbiotic control and creativity. Architecture extends beyond the efforts of architects alone; it is an interdisciplinary activity in which aesthetic, technical, and economic values are tested in a variety of shared spaces for design.

Computer simulations shape the interdisciplinary interactions of designers and, thus, the social organization of their work. Even today, in 2012, designers squabble about the role that simulation software should play in their offices. Among other things, they fight about its role in setting internal hierarchies and choosing external consultants. They bicker about the selection of new simulation software, knowing that choosing software implies greater power for those who are expert in it.

As designers map out their new professional spaces, they use computer simulations to make conceptual distinctions. To identify their ways of using new technologies, designers make trade-offs between the ethic of ultimate ends and the ethic of responsibility. When designers employ simulations to produce performance-based knowledge, they differentiate it from prescriptive knowledge. When designers turn to simulations to articulate the performance of form, they distinguish it from form's intent. Such juxtapositions underlie efforts by designers to create places for themselves in architecture. However, different disciplines bring their own skills, associations, and feelings of purpose to this task.

Architects use simulations in ways that both build upon their traditional abilities, such as drawing, and open up new avenues for aesthetic inquiry. But even among architects, individuals approach simulations with different aptitudes and degrees of comfort. Tim Quix, the CATIA expert introduced at the beginning of this book, has had the opportunity to work with two of the architecture firms I have discussed. He sees Paul Morris and Ralph Jerome as accepting new technologies in different ways, both for their firms and for themselves. Morris is more personally receptive to the computer. When it comes to the machine, Quix says that "[Paul Morris] is better at looking." In contrast, Ralph Jerome, keenly aware and a bit wary of the power of the technology on which his office is building its reputation, refuses to look at his designs on the screen. He says it is like placing his hand in a flame.[262]

Meanwhile, the engineers that I have focused on most acutely make use of simulations to support their roles as collaborative consultants. They acknowledge more explicitly the ways that computer simulations help them to establish exchanges with collaborators, clients, and regulators. They must bridge the technical capabilities of their simulations and the functional, aesthetic, and economic needs of each project. However, for engineers and architects alike, simulations must be both technologically defensible and culturally palatable.

Although this book is an introduction to some of the themes, methods, and goals of studying emerging cultures of computer simulation in architecture, much research remains to be done if we are to understand and respond to changing professional patterns. My study of narratives leaves out a range of voices and concerns. Some of these omissions have already been acknowledged, including the limited geographical and professional scope of practices examined. I have chosen to focus on new technical designers in architecture, in the United States and the United Kingdom. However, I have also left aside a serious discussion about the role of demographics.[263] I have not asked how conceptions of race, class, gender, and other personal differences shape attitudes toward technology in architecture. In matters of professional positioning, these differences make a difference. Amelia Pearce shrugs off the fact that fire safety engineering has had more women than other disciplines at Arup over the years, "probably because men didn't want to do it." When I first started this study, I found that many designers did not want to discuss demographics. Even those who were minorities in their home disciplines insisted that they were treated like everybody else. But what is troubling is that these responses suggest that all personal differences can and should be neutralized; does this mean there are certain demographic positions that designers must conform to?[264]

Indeed, there are clear occasions when expected and actual identities do clash to dramatic effect. This is the case in Amelia Pearce's account of being nominated for "man of the year" in the 1970s by the *Engineering News Record*.[265] She did not win, but she was awarded a bronze plaque that says she was picked from "among many men." However, Pearce laughs this off as well. When I first spoke with her, I accepted such responses with frustration, but little sense about how to approach the issue more productively. As I write this, I am increasingly aware of the defensive motivations behind professional attempts to assume demographic neutrality. In the years since Pearce's nomination, some expectations have changed, but the purported irrelevance of demographic distinctions among designers suggests that difference and its importance are still unacknowledged today.[266] New approaches to research are needed to recognize differences in designers' identities, particularly if a pluralist perspective is to be adopted.[267]

Non-Professional Narratives

No matter how diverse, studies of professional narratives only tell one side of the story of architecture. Taking a symmetrical view, we should also consider the changing narratives of architecture's inhabitants.[268] After all, professionals and non-professionals co-construct the material, experiential, and conceptual reality of buildings and cities. Ideas about architecture among non-professionals are shaped by technologies, just as they are among professionals. In fact, non-professionals face dilemmas similar to their professional counterparts. On identity, they ask: who am I in relation to my surroundings? On knowledge, they wonder: what can I know about the history, safety, and future of the built environment? On form, they consider: what makes a liveable and enjoyable space for dwelling? Although this book does not focus on the conceptions of inhabitants, I would like to chart out that space for future research. What are the simulations that inhabitants use and the cultures they construct in order to clarify their place in architecture? This question suggests that my account of new roles and relationships is only half complete at best. In fact, inhabitants should be thought of as co-designers themselves, generating their own range of personal spatial experiences.[269]

Like the professional designers profiled in this book, inhabitants perceive space through a set of social and technological relationships. I believe, along with city design theorist Kevin Lynch, that inhabitants also make use of narratives to organize these relationships. If we are to understand the extents of contemporary conceptions of space in buildings, cities, and beyond, we should examine how non-professional narratives reveal new configurations of people, machines, and environments.

Lynch popularized the idea that each inhabitant carries around a mental image of his or her city. As a young professor at MIT in the 1950s, Lynch began thinking about cities in terms of their "imageability."[270] He first defined the term in a small, but widely-read book entitled *The Image of the City*, in print consistently by the MIT Press since 1960. "Imageability is that shape, color, or arrangement which facilitates the making of vividly identified, powerfully structured, highly useful mental images of the environment."[271] It is the capacity of architecture to be translated into coherent narratives by professionals and non-professionals alike.[272]

During the writing of this book, *The Image of the City* had its 50th anniversary, making this an opportune time to rethink the notion of imageability in the context of new forms of urban life developing around images produced with computer simulations.[273] Just as Lynch tapped into the narrative models of his time, and helped to identify something of the visual cultures of American cities, I call attention to contemporary narratives about architecture developing within cultures of computer simulation.[274] Taking Lynch's study as a point of departure, here are some new themes for the study of images of cities today.

First, city images are now dynamic, relational, and interactive. In contrast, the images of Lynch's day were static compositions. Although Lynch lamented this representational limitation, particularly in his later book, *What Time is this Place?*, he lacked the tools and techniques to deal with the image of the city in more dimensions.[275] Contemporary digital images of cities redefine imageability by offering perspectives on the city that make time, parallel trajectories, and quantitative data both visible and malleable.

Second, city images are socially and technologically situated in many new ways.[276] Instead of seeking the underlying structural similarities in diverse images of the city, as Lynch did, both public and personal images should be explored. A public image relies on elements shared by all city narratives. I suggest also juxtaposing the diverse personal experiences in cities, rather than averaging them. Cities are imageable in different ways by various inhabitants.

Figure 24 Image from a Cornell University student project by Milena Zindovic, depicting New York City as a fragmented assembly of views from Google Streetview and Google Earth.

Third, city images are more real than ever. One of the underlying motivations of my work has been to examine how notions of "real" architecture are constructed in relationship to computer simulations. Understanding conceptions of the city should not simply be, as it was for Lynch, a precondition to altering the physical city in response. I take seriously the effects of images themselves and the consequences of changing images alone. How can we understand the relationship between dominant, idealized representations of cities, which are widely used and accepted by inhabitants, and everyday experiences? Such disparities often go unnoticed, begging the question: which is more real?

These claims suggest some of the ways that current conceptions of cities depart from the narratives that dominated 50 years ago. New narratives reveal new images. As Jerome Bruner writes, narrative models have the potential to structure not just the telling of stories, but our perceptual experiences of the world.[277] Our cities are becoming the new stories that we tell about them.[278]

The narratives of both professionals and non-professionals in architecture demonstrate some of the richness of studying human–computer–environment relationships. Related studies in other domains can be found in the work of researchers in science, technology, and society (STS), human factors, and distributed cognition.[279] Developments in these fields have contributed enormously to our understanding of what might be called *environmental imaginations*, our collective ways of thinking about our surroundings for purposes ranging from identification and navigation to industry and art. However, architecture is still largely unexamined as a domain for scrutinizing social and technological relationships tightly intertwined with the construction of place.[280] I have tried to make the case for more such studies. Examining human–machine–environment relationships in architecture can help us reflect on the changing meaning of dwelling. We should ask: what do cities, neighborhoods, and homes look like through a socio-technical lens?

This book is the beginning of a conversation about the ways in which architecture is being re-imagined by its participants through the simulations they use and the way they use them. Architecture, its practices and its consequences, cannot be accepted as ready-made in professional work or in everyday life. Professional designers and non-professional inhabitants are in an evolving symbiotic search for the roles and relationships that can bring them greater control over their environments; new technologies for computer simulation do not change this reality, they become players in it. If we are to further our understanding of architecture's persistent flux, we should conduct deeper and more diverse studies of its narratives, as well as what eludes them.

Notes

1 Loukissas, "Keepers of the Geometry."

2 In the chapters that follow, where individuals are quoted at length, or repeatedly within the chapter, the source of the quoted material is included in an endnote (e.g., interview by the author, 2007). In all other instances, it should be assumed that the source is the author's field notes.

3 "Symposium on the Use of Computers."

4 See Ibid., 17. "Where actual realization is a dominating factor [the computer] is not only a great advantage but it is a necessity."

5 Ibid.

6 Ibid.

7 Ibid., 21.

8 Ibid., 1.

9 Ibid., 17.

10 Ibid., 24.

11 In referencing the subjects of my research, I use the terms designers, practitioners, and professionals somewhat interchangeably. I rely on disciplinary terms such as engineer, architect, and acoustician to make more subtle distinctions between subjects. However, these distinctions are much more blurred in practice than we might expect them to be.

12 Many scholars have written about these transformations. For example, see Mindell, *Digital Apollo*. In the 1920s, barnstormer Roscoe Turner flew with a wax mustache and a pet lion named Gilmore. By the end of the 1960s, Apollo astronaut Michael Collins was flying with a rulebook, a slide rule, and a computer. Turner was a showman. Collins was on his way to becoming a scientist. Also see Galison, *Image and Logic*. In the decades following World War II, computer simulations challenged the professional identities of physicists. The first simulators struggled to place themselves within established categories of experiment or theory, eventually altering what it meant to do either one. Also see Turkle *et al.*, *Information Technologies and Professional Identity*.

13 For more on technology and imagination in science and technology studies, see Marcus, *Technoscientific Imaginaries* and Jasanoff and Kim, "Containing the Atom."

14 "Symposium on the Use of Computers," 17. The *Arup Newsletter* includes a set of papers presented at the symposium and notes from an anxious discussion that followed.

15 Ibid., 21.

16 Ibid., 22.

17 For more on the history of modern workers, see Mumford, *Technics and Civilization*. Lewis Mumford argued that the most significant products of mechanization were modern workers in this 1934 history of the machine. The miner, factory worker, and engineer were forms of life conditioned by a new *technic*; an abstract, mathematical conception of space and time that accompanied the development of the clock and other early mechanisms. When

Mumford explained the clock as "not merely a means of keeping track of the hours, but of synchronizing the actions of men," he initiated a dialog about the human implications of technology that continues today.

18 "Symposium on the Use of Computers," 24.

19 Ibid.

20 "Symposium on the Use of Computers." There is a long history of professionals reframing their work around automation in order to focus on what is deemed essential or challenging to humans.

21 Saint, *Architect and Engineer*, 7.

22 Simon, *The Sciences of the Artificial*. Definitions of design are not necessarily more strategic in practice than in academia. Simon's definition made explicit his own strategic goal of defining a science of design that could hold a dominant place in academic institutions.

23 Porter, "Designer's Objects."

24 Wittgenstein, *The Blue and Brown Books*.

25 For studies of architects' models, particularly those that are more open-ended or exploratory in nature, see the doctoral work of Daniel Cardoso; for example, "The Poetics of Automation."

26 For a further exploration of this division, see Robbins, *Why Architects Draw*.

27 There is an extensive literature on positioning in organizational studies. See Harré and Van Langenhove, *Positioning Theory*.

28 For more on the complex composition of technology, see Leo Marx, "Technology."

29 To start with, see the conference proceedings of ACADIA (www.acadia.org), eCAADe (http://www.ecaade.org), CAADRIA (www.caadria.org), and SIGraDi (www.sigradi.org).

30 For an alternative examination of the changing technological culture in architecture, see Picon, *Digital Culture in Architecture*.

31 Helmreich, *Alien Ocean*. Helmreich adopts the phrase "forms of life" from Wittgenstein to describe new working cultures developing around oceanic microbial life forms.

32 See Carpo, *Architecture in the Age of Printing*; and Evans, *The Projective Cast*.

33 Arup, "Journal Essay," 2.

34 "Symposium on the Use of Computers," 22.

35 Ibid., 21.

36 Turkle, *Life on the Screen*, 23.

37 In her trilogy on computers and the human spirit, *The Second Self*, *Life on the Screen*, and most recently, *Alone Together*, Turkle establishes the groundwork for studying technology and self.

38 Sherry Turkle writes (in *Alone Together*, 1) that technology aspires to be the "architect" of our intimacies in an age in which the autonomy of actual architects has been deeply eroded. Will the old meaning of "architect" as the archetypal creator change along with everyday architecture? How will old metaphors and new practices be reconciled by a broader culture?

39 For more about professional knowledge and its recent transformations, see Schön, *The Reflective Practitioner* and Schön, *Educating the Reflective Practitioner*.

40 For more about the limits of using information technologies in design communication, see Lobel, "Building Information."

41 "Symposium on the Use of Computers." Computers actually still require a great deal of "manual" work that often goes unacknowledged. After all, operators use mice, keyboards, and many other manual input devices with computers.

42 I was trained as an architect first. Later, I had training in computing and ethnography. Although I am as much a designer as any of the subjects in this book, I use the third person

in order to discuss designers. I do this in order to reflect on a broad range of practices, of which I am not necessarily a part.

43 See Turkle, *The Inner History of Devices* for more on understanding technology through ethnographies of individual experience.

44 See Geertz, *The Interpretation of Cultures*. A "thick description" is a technical term in ethnography popularized by Geertz.

45 See Latour, *Science in Action* and Downey, *The Machine in Me* as examples.

46 Nader, "Up the Anthropologist."

47 See Murray, *The Architecture of the Italian Renaissance*.

48 See Thompson, *The Soundscape of Modernity*.

49 See Zalewski and Allen, *Shaping Structures*.

50 See Carpo, *Architecture in the Age of Printing*.

51 The process by which numeracy overtook geometry in architecture and engineering was slow and halting. It occurred over many centuries. See Carpo, *Architecture in the Age of Printing*.

52 See Turkle and Schön, *The Athena Project*.

53 CATIA is an acronym for "Computer Aided Three Dimensional Interactive Application."

54 Cuff, *Architecture*.

55 Larson, *Behind the Postmodern Facade*. Vitruvius, *De Architectura* [Ten Books on Architecture].

56 From personal correspondence between Daniel Cardoso and the author.

57 Individual architects will, of course, have different personal styles of relating to simulation. My analysis here is at the intersection of artifact, personal style, and culturally available roles within the profession. See Turkle and Papert, "Epistemological Pluralism and the Revaluation of the Concrete."

58 "Simulation," *Oxford Dictionary of English*.

59 Ibid. "The technique of imitating the behavior of some situation or process (whether economic, military, mechanical, etc.) by means of a suitably analogous situation or apparatus, esp. for the purpose of study or personnel training."

60 See Baudrillard, *Simulacra and Simulation*.

61 See Simon, *The Sciences of the Artificial*, 15.

62 Winsberg, "Models of Success vs. Success of Models," 4.

63 Simon, *The Sciences of the Artificial*.

64 Porter, "Designer's Objects."

65 See Sismondo, "Models, Simulations, and Their Objects" and Winsberg, "Models of Success vs. Success of Models."

66 The anthropologist Clifford Geertz explains the ethnographic lens as an interpretive frame for studying culture. See Geertz, *The Interpretation of Cultures*.

67 Schuman, "Professionalization and the Social Goals of Architects"

68 The system of professionals involved in the design of environments has changed considerably since it was the subject of an intense period of sociological exploration in the 1980s. This period was exemplified by the publication of edited volumes like Knox, *The Design Professions and the Built Environment* and Blau *et al.*, *Professionals and Urban Form*. Today, a network of software and hardware developers has become part of the way design professionals represent problems and make claims to specialized knowledge. The exploration of this new ecology of building professionals may be the next task of professions theory.

69 See Durkheim and Coser, *The Division of Labor in Society*.

70 See Abbott, *The System of Professions*.

71 Andrew Abbott argues that entirely new professions are rarely formed around technologies. When this happens, it is usually after a lengthy period of conflict. For example, he writes (Ibid., 92), "The technology of airplanes revolutionized the tasks of war. Yet the air arm of

the American military became separate from the Army only after an internal battle of several decades, and it lost a similar fight with the Navy."

72 The term "trading zone" is defined in Galison, *Image and Logic*. Simulations cannot be easily separated out from the muddle of communication that happens in trading zones. The trading zones used by design professionals are complex pidgin languages that evolve slowly over time. They include references to many kinds of artifacts and representations, not only computer simulations. Although we cannot completely disentangle trading zones into a set of constituent representations, when we look at projects which incorporate computer simulations, we can see trading zones opening up or shifting in discernible ways. For an alternative treatment of intermediary social artifacts, see "boundary objects" in Star and Griesemer, "Institutional Ecology, 'Translations' and Boundary Objects."

73 Galison, *Image and Logic*, 690.

74 Simon, *The Sciences of the Artificial*, 123.

75 William Mitchell writes about design exploration in *The Logic of Architecture*. Axel Kilian adopts the metaphor in his dissertation, "Design Exploration through Bidirectional Modeling of Constraints." Terry Knight's course at MIT on Inquiry into Computation and Design inspired me to investigate this metaphor in further depth.

76 Wright, *Frank Lloyd Wright Collected Writings*, 275.

77 See Sheldon, "Digital Surface Representation and the Constructibility of Gehry's Architecture" and Malkawi and Augenbroe, *Advanced Building Simulation*.

78 Heidegger, *The Question Concerning Technology, and other Essays*.

79 Turkle and Papert, "Epistemological Pluralism and the Revaluation of the Concrete."

80 Schön, *The Reflective Practitioner*.

81 Galison, *Image and Logic*, 691.

82 Sismondo, "Models, Simulations, and Their Objects."

83 Ibid., 254.

84 See MacKenzie and Wajcman, *The Social Shaping of Technology* and Bijker *et al.*, *The Social Construction of Technological Systems*.

85 Fablon was developed under the supervision of Alistair Day. However, it is unclear who first implemented it in computer code. The first program for dynamic relaxation at Arup was probably done on punch card computers. Later, Fablon was coded in the computer language C for use on a Sun SPARC workstation.

86 The output was also most likely a text file.

87 See Winsberg, *Science in the Age of Computer Simulation*.

88 See the work of George Stiny for an extensive critique of discrete symbolic computation. In *Shape*, he illustrates how computing with shapes can allow for ambiguities not permitted in symbol manipulation.

89 Winsberg, *Science in the Age of Computer Simulation*, 8.

90 Winsberg, *Science in the Age of Computer Simulation*.

91 Pierre Moreau, interview by the author, 2007.

92 Ibid.

93 "Symposium on the Use of Computers," 5.

94 Ibid.

95 Patrick McCormack, interview by the author, 2007.

96 For example, early on in the history of the Lighting Design Group, Julian Butler used Fortran to code some of his own programs for daylight analysis on UNIX Sun workstations. He produced early renderings using finite element methods. In the mid-1990s, he started to incorporate ray tracing in addition to finite element techniques. Eventually, Radiance became the principal analytical tool for lighting analysis at Arup. Modification and adjustment through scripting still happen in areas like lighting design, where Arup does not

typically develop the base simulations any more. Even if Arup lighting designers no longer write their own software, they frequently write scripts that extend or automate commercial simulations like Radiance.

97 "Symposium on the Use of Computers," 6.
98 Barrett Chapman, interview by the author, 2007.
99 David Turner, interview by the author, 2007.
100 McCormack was trained as a civil engineer. At university, he had limited engagement with computers. He used punch cards to run several structural analysis programs on an old HP computer. Computers were part of Turner's education to a very limited extent. His course required only a little bit of programming, but he had a particular interest in computers and had already learned to program on his own.
101 Turner explains that although Oasys sells its software externally, they first develop software for Arup internally, then sell it. It does not often work the other way around. The development of software is usually driven by some demand that has occurred inside the firm. For instance, in tunnel settlement work there was a need to refine the software to provide damage assessment to buildings as a result of tunnel excavation. The project team devoted both time and financial resources to improving the software.
102 Keller, *Making Sense of Life.*
103 Ibid.
104 Halden Harrison, interview by the author, 2006.
105 See Turkle, *Life on the Screen.*
106 Ibid.
107 Rikle Shales, interview by the author, 2005.
108 Robert Laird, interview by the author, 2005.
109 See Turing, "Computing Machinery and Intelligence" and Turing, "On Computable Numbers, with an Application to the Entscheidungsproblem."
110 See Cuff, *Architecture*, Schön, *The Reflective Practitioner*, and Schön, *Educating the Reflective Practitioner.*
111 Schön, *The Reflective Practitioner*, 80.
112 Banham, "A Black Box," 298.
113 Drew Thorndike, interview by the author, 2005.
114 Merleau-Ponty, *Phenomenology of Perception.*
115 See Forsythe and Hess, *Studying Those Who Study Us.*
116 The phrase "frozen ideology" was used by William Mitchell in a personal conversation with the author in 2005.
117 Downey, *The Machine in Me.*
118 Foucault, *Discipline & Punish*, 94.
119 Turkle, *Alone Together*, 19.
120 For a more elaborate explanation of the development of Sabine's equation, see Thompson, *The Soundscape of Modernity*, 41.
121 Francis Martin, interview by the author, 2006.
122 Ibid.
123 Thompson, *The Soundscape of Modernity.*
124 Ibid., 15.
125 See Weber, *From Max Weber.*
126 Ibid., 121.
127 See Norberg-Schulz, *Architecture: Meaning and Place.*
128 Francis Martin, interview by the author, 2006.
129 Made anonymous for the protection of the subject.
130 Aldus Barnes, interview by the author, 2007.

131 Aldus Barnes, interview by the author, 2007.
132 Made anonymous for the protection of the subject.
133 Richard Wells, interview by the author, 2007. CAD stands for computer-aided design.
134 According to Wells, computational fluid dynamics (CFD) analysis is especially useful for curved glass facades, as in the example of a double-paned model in his studio. When the air inside this curved design heats up and expands, "strange things happen" that can break the glass.
135 Andrew Werner, interview by the author, 2007.
136 For an in-depth analysis of the history of fire safety in buildings, see Wermiel, *The Fireproof Building*.
137 Amelia Pearce, interview by the author, 2007.
138 Talcott Saunders, interview by the author, 2007.
139 Although train stations have long housed large halls, notes Pearce, they are usually so lofty and open that smoke does not present a problem.
140 Made anonymous for the protection of the subject.
141 For more on Stansted Airport, see Powell *et al.*, *Stansted*.
142 Amelia Pearce, interview by the author, 2007.
143 Ibid.
144 See Woods, *From Craft to Profession*.
145 Ibid. During the eighteenth and early nineteenth centuries, building design was taught and practiced as a craft. There was no equivalent of the French *École des Beaux Arts* (architecture school) in the United States. The practices of this era became a foundation for the emergence of a profession.
146 These terms for knowledge are appropriated from Berger and Luckmann, *The Social Construction of Reality*.
147 Integrating design knowledge in computers is often called "building information modeling" or BIM. See Deutsch, *BIM and Integrated Design* and Eastman *et al.*, *BIM Handbook*.
148 Malcolm Dietrich, interview by the author, 2005.
149 From an internal memo at Arup, made anonymous for the protection of the subject.
150 Bloor, *Knowledge and Social Imagery*, 5.
151 Mathew Webb, interview by the author, 2007.
152 Andrew Werner, interview by the author, 2007.
153 Made anonymous for the protection of the subject.
154 See Turkle *et. al.*, *Information Technologies and Professional Identity* for a lengthy explanation of this fear of seduction across a range of disciplines.
155 Halden Harrison, interview by the author, 2006.
156 This is not a straightforward distinction. Veracity must be culturally established as well. In this context, validity is a matter of cultural appeal outside of the technical or scientific community. For further explanation, see Goodman, *Ways of Worldmaking*, 125–129.
157 Some of these assumptions are standardized. In the case of energy modeling, Ashrae is an example of a standard that aids designers in calibrating their simulations by prescribing acceptable inputs and outputs. However, standards are constantly being revised. Figures like those offered by Ashrae are often considered conservative or even outdated by practitioners.
158 Saunders has updated his position as follows: "In discussing evacuation simulation – modeling of flow is straightforward and it is possible to model speed and physical attributes. The more challenging issue is modeling human behaviour because of differences between people and the changes over time attributed to experience. For example, before 9/11 it was often difficult to get occupants of a building to move upon hearing a fire alarm. Post 9/11, especially in tall buildings, this is not so much of an issue. Of course over time

it is likely that people will revert to pre 9/11 behaviour." Talcott Saunders, e-mail correspondence with the author.

159 Haden Bailey, interview by the author, 2007.

160 Turkle *et. al.*, *Information Technologies and Professional Identity*.

161 Christopher Huang, interview by the author, 2006.

162 Today, architects also use many rendering tools; however, these are generally non-analytical, according to Julian Butler of the Arup Lighting Group in London. Architects know that their tools are not photometrically correct, says Butler. He explains that a typical problem with architects' software, like 3D Studio Max, is that it will not calculate light precisely, primarily because it is computationally intensive to render things properly. Architects' tools often leave out the details of the light fixture, the materials, the place, time, etc. In addition, making an accurate simulation is dependent on refinement, like knowing where are the critical areas to increase the computational mesh, the resolution of the analysis.

163 However, according to Watson Richards, "software like 3ds Max is now capable of doing accurate lighting analysis." He and his colleague Anthony Cortez demonstrated this at an Autodesk Master Class at the SIGGRAPH 2006 conference. He remarks: "It uses photometric lights, renders in 16 or 32 bit file formats and its material functions allow accurate reflectance and transmittance values to be adjusted and set, [the] same as Radiance. It's closing the gap very rapidly as a valid simulation software." Watson Richards, e-mail correspondence with the author, 2008.

164 "I've been part of a concerted effort to integrate various disciplines' models within Arup and several strides have been made since you conducted your research – we can now adapt BIM models such as CATIA, Revit, Solidworks, etc[.] into 3DS Max for Visualization. Navisworks is now used as a common destination for most BIM models. Realtime Quest models now work with our Acoustic Team[']s CATTwalker (Realtime Acoustic software), etc. And the objective of the new Arup SoundLab under development is to be more of an integrated simulation room. I don't see us heading towards a single integrated model but rather a common set of transfer formats that allow us to utilize the same model (or parts of it) in different software depending on the need." Watson Richards, e-mail correspondence with the author, 2008.

165 Clemens Atkinson, interview by the author, 2007.

166 Gropius, *Scope of Total Architecture*.

167 Ove Arup's personal and professional archive can be found at Churchill College in Cambridge University.

168 Edward Malone, interview by the author, 2006.

169 William Porter notes that there used to be a single integrating simulation: the architect's drawings and specifications. All consultant data would be fed into these. A conflict between drawings and specifications would typically be resolved in favor of the specifications.

170 For instance, Pearce's approach was used by Arup Fire to reduce costs for Columbia University in fire-resistant paint on the Learner Student Center, a glass and steel building designed by Bernard Tschumi, then dean of Columbia's Architecture Department. By regulation, all of the exposed steel should have been painted to retard the effect of a fire on the structural integrity of the building. Arup's simulations convinced building regulators and the fire brigade in New York that the intent of these regulations could be met through alternative means, primarily through redundancy in the structure. The Arup Fire Group in London used simulations to illustrate the specific, contingent experience of a virtual fire in the Learner Student Center. The performance-based knowledge of their simulations substituted for prescriptive notions about how buildings in New York City should be built.

171 Adrian Ball, from written correspondence with the author, 2008.

172 Forty, *Words and Buildings*.

173 Ibid., 161.

174 Simon, *The Sciences of the Artificial*. This articulation of a shared space of design also owes something to Latour, *Aramis, or the Love of Technology*, which explains the development and eventual failure of a French transit project in terms of the struggle of its designers to converge upon a shared narrative.

175 See pluralism in Turkle and Papert, "Epistemological Pluralism and the Revaluation of the Concrete" and de Certeau, *The Practice of Everyday Life*.

176 For an alternative exploration of pluralism in large-scale design, see Appleyard, *Planning a Pluralist City*.

177 Drew Thorndike, interview by the author, 2005.

178 NURBS stands for non-uniform rational b-spline.

179 Drew Thorndike, interview by the author, 2005.

180 One of the earliest uses of this aphorism was in Sullivan, "The Tall Office Building Artistically Considered."

181 Messent, *Opera House Act One*, 260.

182 Ibid.

183 Arup was hired directly by the Opera House client, the Ministry of Public Works in New South Wales.

184 Messent, *Opera House Act One*.

185 Ibid.

186 Jørn Utzon eventually resigned from the project under pressure from the Ministry of Public Works.

187 Messent, *Opera House Act One*, 223.

188 See Taffs, "Computers and the Opera House."

189 For an in-depth study of concrete from a social perspective, see Slaton, *Reinforced Concrete and the Modernization of American Building, 1900–1930*.

190 Murray, *The Saga of Sydney Opera House*.

191 Ibid., 30.

192 Ibid., 35.

193 Ibid., 30.

194 Messent, *Opera House Act One*, 222.

195 Forty, *Words and Buildings*.

196 Ibid., 150.

197 Pogrebin, "Extreme Makeover, Museum Edition."

198 From an Arup report to the Wexner Center administration.

199 Christopher Huang, interview by the author, 2006.

200 Forty, *Words and Buildings*, 168.

201 Ibid.

202 Arup was originally hired to perform an analysis on a proposed renovation of the space designed by a local firm. However, Arup engineers were appalled when they saw the proposed scheme. Local engineers were suggesting highly unconventional and risky quick fixes for the problems of the museum. Arup told the museum that, for a little more money, a new system could be installed. The museum eventually hired Arup to redesign the curtain wall and other building systems.

203 Pogrebin, "Extreme Makeover, Museum Edition."

204 The Arup team used a combination of computational fluid dynamics modeling and a full mock-up of the facade to test the thermal performance of the windows. They also considered the results of airflow simulation software developed by the Lawrence Berkeley National Laboratory because traditional CFD could not mesh fine enough to simulate thermal leakage on the Wexner Center windows.

205 Forty, *Words and Buildings.*

206 Ibid., 160.

207 Pogrebin, "Extreme Makeover, Museum Edition."

208 One foot-candle is the illuminance on a one square foot surface under a uniformly distributed flux of one lumen.

209 Thomson, *The Museum Environment.*

210 Oscar Davis, comments made in a lecture at MIT on April 4, 2008.

211 The importance of illuminance values in contemporary museums recalls the focus on reverberation time in concert halls at the beginning of the twentieth century. At that time, the Sabine equation, a simple formula for estimating the reverberation time of sound in buildings opened a new numerically oriented exchange between architects and acousticians (see also Chapter 3, "The acoustician"). Measures like illuminance and reverberation time represent performance in quantitative terms, amenable to simple comparison and control. However, there is a danger that numerically oriented approaches can be aesthetically narrowing. Historically, they have led to cultures of optimization and homogeneity.

212 William Porter, comments made from the audience of a lecture by Oscar Davis at MIT on April 4, 2008.

213 Michael Cullen, interview by the author, 2007.

214 Ibid.

215 Using Sun SPARC workstations with 24 megabytes of ram and 386 processors.

216 One problem with such lighting simulations is that they can never duplicate the level of contrast in a real scene. Direct sun in the summer can reach 10,000 foot-candles. The blinding experience of looking into the sun cannot be replicated by an image. At the time, however, Arup's renderings were convincing enough. The images were accepted as predictors of visual experience in the Mercedes studios. Today, our expectations of virtual reality are much different.

217 Francis Martin, interview by the author, 2006.

218 Thompson, *The Soundscape of Modernity*, 324.

219 In an e-mail in August 2008, Francis Martin clarifies how Arup became part of the discussion about acoustics at Alice Tully Hall. "We were specifically chosen for this peer review role because (a) the client had visited the Arup SoundLab and listened to demonstrations of possible modifications to the acoustics of the Avery Fisher Hall and had successfully implemented one of them (b) they needed a second opinion on some of the design measures being proposed to test their validity and subjective value against cost and (c) Arup was the structural and mechanical engineer for the refurbishment project. They came to us because we had tools that no one else had."

220 Linus Russell, interview by the author, 2006.

221 Francis Martin, interview by the author, 2006.

222 Ibid.

223 Reddy, "The Conduit Metaphor."

224 Norberg-Schulz, *Architecture.*

225 Francis Martin, interview by the author, 2006.

226 For an explanation of the origins of perspective, see Ivins, *On the Rationalization of Sight.*

227 Thompson, *The Soundscape of Modernity*, 324.

228 "Anybody can build a building," says David Turner of Arup, "but it takes an engineer to make it economical." Simulations present engineers with new avenues toward discovering the most economical design. With the use of auralization, the calculation of economic value in acoustics has become a matter of evaluating experience.

229 Francis Martin, interview by the author, 2006.

230 Habraken and Gross, *Concept Design Games.*

231 Ibid.

232 Each game has a technical universe, a site, a program, roles, moves, goals, protocols, and a scoring system. See Habraken and Gross, *Concept Design Games* for more detail on how to develop new games.

233 When I first played The Silent Game in William Porter's "Design Inquiry" course at MIT, we assembled forms out of Lego bricks. The Silent Game requires three players: A, B, and the observer. There are also three rounds of play, each lasting five minutes, followed by a discussion. In the first round, player A has five minutes to create a composition, usually with some regulating idea in mind (for example, create an ascending spiral, use only 2 × 6 red blocks, etc.). During this time, player B and the observer are looking on. In the second round, player B has five minutes to add, subtract, modify, or in some way respond to player A's composition without speaking (for example, create smaller tangent spirals, place additional 2 × 6 red blocks, etc.). This time, player A and the observer watch. In the final round, player A has a chance to make a counter response by further altering the composition. Finally, each of the three players has an opportunity to reveal their personal interpretation of events verbally. The observer speaks first, followed by player B, then player A. They each try to explain player A's idea, player B's response, and the counter response from player A. These reflections often diverge in unexpected ways, revealing the differences in attention, interests, and biases among the players. The game has many possible analogies to real-world design. Player A could be thought of as a master architect and player B his or her apprentice. The reverse is also plausible, if we see the actions of Player B as corrections on Player A's work. The two players could also be client and designer or even architect and engineer. The Silent Game can be tweaked to make such roles more pronounced.

234 Habraken, discussion with the author, 2011.

235 For a discussion of matters of fact and matters of concern, see Latour, *Reassembling the Social*.

236 Many ethnographies of architecture have been done before. Cuff, *Architecture*, is one of the best known. For a recent example that takes a socio-technical perspective, see Yaneva, *The Making of a Building*.

237 See Bruner, "Life as Narrative."

238 Complexity is in the eye of the beholder. George Stiny's work on Shape Grammars illustrates this well. See Stiny, *Shape*.

239 Bernard, *Research Methods in Anthropology*.

240 See Haraway, "Situated Knowledges."

241 See literature on constructivist approaches to knowledge: Goodman, *Ways of Worldmaking* and Ackermann, "Perspective-taking and Object Construction."

242 Geertz, *The Interpretation of Cultures*, 15.

243 Cited by Bruner, "Life as Narrative," 691.

244 See Bruner, ibid., 696, as well as his references on Russian formalists; Kermode, "Secrets and Narrative Sequence"; and Propp, *Morphology of the Folktale*.

245 The objectification of experience by design professionals is not new. See Ivins, *On the Rationalization of Sight*. Ivins explains how modern notions of sight developed in Renaissance Europe through the invention of linear perspective. The "perspectival" system is a framework for creating optical consistency among images. It allows artists to construct fantastic images that share the same structure as representations of nature. Through the use of perspective, fantasy can appear as believable as reality. Since the Renaissance, rationalization has been extended to many other areas of perceptual and spatial experience.

246 Pierre Moreau, interview by the author, 2007.

247 Alvin Bernard, interview by the author, 2007.

248 Francis Martin, interview by the author, 2006.

249 Aldus Barnes, interview by the author, 2007.

250 Many who have written about architecture have invoked theater, but for different purposes. See the work of Lewis Mumford and Sebastiano Serlio as examples.

251 Architectural theory has of course made use of Brecht's work. In *House III*, Peter Eisenman presents a dialogical building in the tradition of Brecht. Eisenman uses Brecht to think about how architecture might be experienced from a critical perspective. See Davidson and Allen, *Tracing Eisenman.*

252 Krasner, *Theatre in Theory, 1900–2000.*

253 Baudrillard, *Simulacra and Simulation*, 2.

254 Krasner, *Theatre in Theory, 1900–2000.*

255 Talcott Saunders, interview with the author, 2007.

256 Brecht, *Brecht on Theatre.*

257 Ibid., 37.

258 Ibid., 71.

259 Latour, *Science in Action.*

260 Ibid.

261 Narratives in a range of complex environments, including aviation, space exploration, undersea science, and warfare are being reshaped by computer simulations. See the ongoing work of the MIT Laboratory for Automation, Robotics, and Society.

262 Source made anonymous to protect the identity of the subject.

263 Thanks to Zara Mirmalek for suggesting the use of the term "demographics" to account for this set of concerns.

264 See literature on gender in technical work including Jorgenson, "Engineering Selves" and Wajcman, "Reflections on Gender and Technology Studies."

265 Amelia Pearce, from an interview by the author, 2007.

266 See work by Steven Epstein on difference in social studies of technology; for example, Epstein, *Impure Science.*

267 There is some literature on gender, race, and class in architecture, but rarely in relationship to the technologies of design. See Colomina and Bloomer, *Sexuality & Space.*

268 I do not like the word "users," because it underplays the constructionist role of inhabitants in the creation of architecture. For more about the symmetrical approach to social studies of technology, see Latour, *Science in Action.*

269 See de Certeau, *The Practice of Everyday Life.*

270 Lynch developed the idea of imageability in close dialog with the visual artist György Kepes.

271 Lynch, *The Image of the City*, 9.

272 Architect Mark Wigley writes, "the sense of sequential narrative as the basis for orientation organizes Lynch's work . . ." Wigley, "Lost in Space," 46.

273 Numerous media scholars are writing about how human presence is being redefined through the use of computer simulation. Sherry Turkle sees the self, now incomplete without its devices, as occupying "a liminal space between the physical real and its lives on the screen." Having computing both always on and always on you evokes "a sense of continual co-presence." I have been expanding this inquiry in order to examine human presence at scales beyond individual relationships, to look at presence in cities and other complex environments. See Turkle, "Always-on/Always-on-you," 122, Williams and Dourish, "Reimagining the City," Mitchell, *Me++*, and Shepard, *Sentient City*. See my own work in this area, done in collaboration with John Zissovici and students at Cornell University, at www.surfacecities.com (Angel Dust, 2009).

274 Lynch acknowledges the power of image-making technologies in his book. "Since image development is a two-way process between observer and observed, it is possible to

strengthen the image either by symbolic devices, by the retraining of the perceiver, or by reshaping one's surroundings." Lynch, *The Image of the City*, 11.

275 Lynch, *What Time is this Place?*

276 Lynch was interested in the effect of technology on thought processes. Although he raised this issue in *The Image of the City*, he addressed it head-on in Appleyard *et al.*, *The View from the Road.*, where he considered how conceptions of the city are framed by the automobile. My study diverges most profoundly from Lynch's study in my choice of subjects. Lynch saw inhabitants' conceptual maps as distorted images to be compared to more objectively defined images developed by professionals, like himself and his students. I am interested in the distortions in professional images of architecture. Lynch looked for some kind of average narrative, the lowest common denominator among accounts of the city. (Although he knew this was problematic.) My study has focused on unusual and transformative narratives that help us see architecture in new ways, through the lenses of technology.

277 Bruner, "Life as Narrative."

278 Today's digital tools can also allow us to present narratives visually. Data visualizations are not immersive simulations, but in their own way, they can be aids to collective imagination. As representations of inhabitants and their narratives, data visualizations can help a range of audiences see new patterns in architecture using massive amounts of social data collected by census or by sensors. See the work of the MIT SENSEable City Lab for visualization projects that build on Lynch's work, often using sensor and cell-phone data; for example, Morello and Ratti, "A Digital Image of the City." However, with the growing surplus of quantitative approaches to urban analysis, it is also important to continue the qualitative, interview-based studies of cities that Lynch pioneered.

279 Science, technology, and society or STS (also known as science and technology studies) is an emerging discipline that traces the social, cultural, and political dimensions of scientific knowledge and technology. Scholars in STS apply methods from sociology, anthropology, history, and philosophy to the study of technical domains. They show how even the hardest technical facts are established through social processes. See Bloor, *Knowledge and Social Imagery*. But just as importantly for my own study, STS scholars illustrate how everyday social interactions are mediated by the epistemological framing of contemporary science and technology. See Turkle, *Alone Together*. "Human factors" is a sub-discipline of engineering that examines the role of people in technological systems. Conventional studies of human factors focus on individual operators, emphasizing attention, ergonomics, and workload. See Sheridan, *Humans and Automation*. However, the organization of human–machine groups, and the negotiation of control, and the role of place are largely unexamined. Meanwhile, these social dimensions have consequences for decision-making at technical and policy levels. Distributed cognition is an area of study on the boundary between cognitive science and anthropology (sometimes called cognitive anthropology) that seeks to map the microphysics of social and technological systems. This discipline acknowledges that in any decision-making system, internal (mental) processes and external (cultural) processes are divided among humans, machines, and environmental features. See Hutchins, *Cognition in the Wild*.

280 For more on architecture and STS, see Galison and Thompson, *The Architecture of Science*, Eigen, "Between Stations and Habitations," and Gieryn, "A Space for Place in Sociology."

Bibliography

Abbott, Andrew. *The System of Professions: An Essay on the Division of Expert Labor.* 1st ed. Chicago, IL: University of Chicago Press, 1988.

Ackermann, Edith. "Perspective-taking and Object Construction." In *Constructionism in Practice: Designing, Thinking, and Learning in a Digital World,* edited by Yasmin Kafai and Mitchel Resnick. Mahwah, NJ: Lawrence Erlbaum Associates, 1996: 25–37.

Appleyard, Donald. *Planning a Pluralist City: Conflicting Realities in Ciudad Guayana.* Cambridge, MA: The MIT Press, 1976.

Appleyard, Donald, Lynch, Kevin, and Myer, John Randolph. *The View from the Road.* Published for the Joint Center for Urban Studies of the Massachusetts Institute of Technology and Harvard University. Cambridge, MA: The MIT Press, 1964.

Arup, Ove. "Journal Essay." 5 (September 3, 1970). London: Arup.

Banham, Reyner. "A Black Box: The Secret Profession of Architecture." In *A Critic Writes: Selected Essays by Reyner Banham.* Berkeley, CA: University of California Press, 1996: 292–300.

Baudrillard, Jean. *Simulacra and Simulation.* Ann Arbor: University of Michigan Press, 1995.

Berger, Peter L., and Luckmann, Thomas. *The Social Construction of Reality: A Treatise in the Sociology of Knowledge.* New York, NY: Doubleday, 1966.

Bernard, Russell H. *Research Methods in Anthropology: Qualitative and Quantitative Approaches.* Thousand Oaks, CA: Sage Publications, 1995.

Bijker, Wiebe E., Hughes, Thomas P., and Pinch, Trevor. *The Social Construction of Technological Systems: New Directions in the Sociology and History of Technology.* Cambridge, MA: The MIT Press, 1989.

Blau, Judith R., Gory, Mark L. A., and Pipkin, John S. *Professionals and Urban Form.* New York: State University of New York Press, 1983.

Bloor, David. *Knowledge and Social Imagery.* Chicago, IL: University of Chicago Press, 1991.

Brecht, Bertolt. *Brecht on Theatre: The Development of an Aesthetic.* 13th ed. New York, NY: Hill and Wang, 1977.

Bruner, Jerome. "Life as Narrative." *Social Research* 71(3) (Fall 2004): 691–710.

Cardoso, Daniel. "The Poetics of Automation: Conceptions of Human and Non-Human Agency in Design." Paper presented at the 4S (Society for the Social Studies of Science) Conference, Tokyo, 2010.

Carpo, Mario. *Architecture in the Age of Printing: Orality, Writing, Typography, and Printed Images in the History of Architectural Theory.* Cambridge, MA: The MIT Press, 2001.

Colomina, Beatriz, and Bloomer, Jennifer. *Sexuality & Space.* Princeton, NJ: Princeton Architectural Press, 1992.

Cuff, Dana. *Architecture: The Story of Practice.* Cambridge, MA: The MIT Press, 1991.

Davidson, Cynthia C., and Allen, Stan. *Tracing Eisenman: Peter Eisenman Complete Works.* New York, NY: Rizzoli, 2006.

de Certeau, Michel. *The Practice of Everyday Life.* 2nd ed. Berkeley, CA: University of California Press, 2002.

Deutsch, Randy. *BIM and Integrated Design: Strategies for Architectural Practice*. 1st ed. Hoboken, NJ: Wiley, 2011.

Downey, Gary Lee. *The Machine in Me: An Anthropologist Sits among Computer Engineers*. 1st ed. New York, NY: Routledge, 1998.

Durkheim, Emile, and Coser, Lewis A. *The Division of Labor in Society*. New York, NY: Free Press, 1997.

Eastman, Chuck, Teicholz, Paul, Sacks, Rafael, and Liston, Kathleen. *BIM Handbook: A Guide to Building Information Modeling for Owners, Managers, Designers, Engineers and Contractors*. 2nd ed. Hoboken, NJ: Wiley, 2011.

Eigen, Edward. "Between Stations and Habitations: the Architecture of French Science at the Shore, 1830–1900." Thesis, Massachusetts Institute of Technology, 2000. Available at http://dspace.mit.edu/handle/1721.1/49795?show=full.

Epstein, Steven. *Impure Science: AIDS, Activism, and the Politics of Knowledge*. Berkeley, CA: University of California Press, 1998.

Evans, Robin. *The Projective Cast: Architecture and Its Three Geometries*. Cambridge, MA: The MIT Press, 2000.

Forsythe, Diana E., and Hess, David J. *Studying Those Who Study Us: An Anthropologist in the World of Artificial Intelligence*. 1st ed. Stanford, CA: Stanford University Press, 2002.

Forty, Adrian. *Words and Buildings: A Vocabulary of Modern Architecture*. New York, NY: Thames & Hudson, 2004.

Foucault, Michel. *Discipline & Punish: The Birth of the Prison*. 2nd ed. New York, NY: Vintage, 1995.

Galison, Peter Louis. *Image and Logic: A Material Culture of Microphysics*. 1st ed. Chicago, IL: University of Chicago Press, 1997.

Galison, Peter, and Thompson, Emily. *The Architecture of Science*. Cambridge, MA: The MIT Press, 1999.

Geertz, Clifford. *The Interpretation of Cultures: Selected Essays*. 1st ed. New York, NY: Basic Books, 1973.

Gieryn, Thomas F. "A Space for Place in Sociology." *Annual Review of Sociology* 26(1) (August 2000): 463–496.

Goodman, Nelson. *Ways of Worldmaking*. Indianapolis, IN: Hackett Publishing Company, 1978.

Gropius, Walter. *Scope of Total Architecture*. New York, NY: Collier Books, 1962.

Habraken, John, and Gross, Mark. *Concept Design Games*. A report submitted to the National Science Foundation. Cambridge, MA: MIT Department of Architecture, 1987.

Haraway, Donna. "Situated Knowledges: The Science Question in Feminism and the Privilege of Partial Perspective." *Feminist Studies* 14(3) (1988): 575–599.

Harré, Rom, and Van Langenhove, Luk (Eds). *Positioning Theory: Moral Contexts of International Action*. 1st ed. Hoboken, NJ: Wiley-Blackwell, 1998.

Heidegger, Martin. *The Question Concerning Technology, and Other Essays*. New York, NY: Harper & Row, 1977.

Helmreich, Stefan. *Alien Ocean: Anthropological Voyages in Microbial Seas*. Berkeley: University of California Press, 2009.

Hutchins, Edwin. *Cognition in the Wild*. Cambridge, MA: The MIT Press, 1996.

Ivins, William M., Jr. *On the Rationalization of Sight; With an Examination of Three Renaissance Texts on Perspective*. New York, NY: Da Capo Press, 1973.

Jasanoff, Sheila, and Kim, Sang-Hyun. "Containing the Atom: Sociotechnical Imaginaries and Nuclear Power in the United States and South Korea." *Minerva* 47(2) (June 2009): 119–146.

Jorgenson, Jane. "Engineering Selves." *Management Communication Quarterly* 15(3) (February 1, 2002): 350–380.

Keller, Evelyn Fox. *Making Sense of Life: Explaining Biological Development with Models, Metaphors, and Machines*. Cambridge, MA: Harvard University Press, 2003.

Kermode, Frank. "Secrets and Narrative Sequence." In *On Narrative*, edited by W. J. T. Mitchell. Chicago, IL: University of Chicago Press, 1984.

Kilian, Axel. "Design Exploration through Bidirectional Modeling of Constraints." Thesis, Massachusetts Institute of Technology, 2006. Available at http://dspace.mit.edu/handle/1721.1/33803.

Knox, Paul L. *The Design Professions and the Built Environment*. Dubuque, IA: Nichols Publishing Company, 1988.

Krasner, David. *Theatre in Theory, 1900–2000: An Anthology*. Oxford, UK: Blackwell Publishing, 2008.

Larson, Magali Sarfatti. *Behind the Postmodern Facade: Architectural Change in Late Twentieth-Century America*. Berkeley, CA: University of California Press, 1995.

Latour, Bruno. *Science in Action: How to Follow Scientists and Engineers through Society*. Cambridge, MA: Harvard University Press, 1987.

—— *Aramis, or the Love of Technology*. Cambridge, MA: Harvard University Press, 1996.

—— *Reassembling the Social: An Introduction to Actor–Network–Theory*. Oxford, UK: Oxford University Press, 2008.

Lobel, Joshua M. "Building Information: Means and Methods of Communication in Design and Construction." Thesis, Massachusetts Institute of Technology, 2006. Available at http://dspace.mit.edu/handle/1721.1/43747?show=full.

Loukissas, Yanni. "Keepers of the Geometry." In *Simulation and Its Discontents*, edited by Sherry Turkle. Cambridge, MA: The MIT Press, 2009: 153–170.

Lynch, Kevin. *What Time is this Place?* Cambridge, MA: The MIT Press, 1972.

—— *The Image of the City*. Cambridge, MA: The MIT Press, 1992.

MacKenzie, Donald, and Wajcman, Judy. *The Social Shaping of Technology*. 2nd ed. Buckingham, UK: McGraw Hill Education /Open University Press, 1999.

Malkawi, Ali, and Augenbroe, Godfried. *Advanced Building Simulation*. New York, NY: Spon Press, 2004.

Marcus, George E. *Technoscientific Imaginaries: Conversations, Profiles, and Memoirs*. 1st ed. Chicago, IL: University of Chicago Press, 1995.

Marx, Leo. "Technology: The Emergence of a Hazardous Concept." *Technology and Culture* 51(3) (2010): 561–577.

Merleau-Ponty, Maurice. *Phenomenology of Perception*. New York, NY: Routledge, 2002.

Messent, David. *Opera House Act One*. Sydney: David Messent Photography, 1997.

Mindell, David. *Digital Apollo: Human and Machine in Spaceflight*. Cambridge, MA: The MIT Press, 2008.

Mitchell, William J. *Me++: The Cyborg Self and the Networked City*. Cambridge, MA: The MIT Press, 2004.

Mitchell, William John. *The Logic of Architecture: Design, Computation, and Cognition*. Cambridge, MA: The MIT Press, 1990.

Morello, Eugenio, and Ratti, Carlo. "A Digital Image of the City: 3D Isovists in Lynch's Urban Analysis." *Environment and Planning B: Planning and Design* 36(5) (2009): 837–853.

Mumford, Lewis. *Technics and Civilization*. Chicago, IL: University of Chicago Press, 2010 [1934].

Murray, Peter. *The Architecture of the Italian Renaissance*. Rei Sub ed. New York, NY: Schocken Books, 1997.

—— *The Saga of Sydney Opera House: The Dramatic Story of the Design and Construction of the Icon of Modern Australia*. London: Spon Press, 2004.

Nader, Laura. "Up the Anthropologist: Perspectives Gained from Studying Up." In *Reinventing Anthropology*, edited by Dell Hymes. New York, NY: Pantheon Press, 1972: 285–311.

Norberg-Schulz, Christian. *Architecture: Meaning and Place: Selected Essays*. New York, NY: Rizzoli International Publications, 1988.

Picon, Antoine. *Digital Culture in Architecture*. 1st ed. Basel: Birkhäuser Architecture, 2010.

Pogrebin, Robin. "Extreme Makeover, Museum Edition." *The New York Times* (September 18, 2005), design section.

Porter, William L. "Designer's Objects." In *Design Representation*, edited by Gabriela Goldschmidt and William L. Porter. New York, NY: Springer, 2010: 63–79.

Powell, Ken, Bryant, Richard, and Sayer, Philip. *Stansted: Norman Foster and the Architecture of Flight*. London, UK: Fourth Estate, 1992.

Propp, Vladimir. *Morphology of the Folktale*. Austin, TX: University of Texas Press, 1968.

Reddy, Michael. "The Conduit Metaphor." In *Metaphor and Thought*, edited by Andrew Ortony. Cambridge, UK: Cambridge University Press, 1993: 164–201.

Robbins, Edward. *Why Architects Draw*. Cambridge, MA: The MIT Press, 1994.

Saint, Andrew. *Architect and Engineer: A Study in Sibling Rivalry*. New Haven, CT: Yale University Press, 2008.

Saunders, George. *A Treatise on Theatres*. London: I. and J. Taylor, 1790.

Schuman, Tony. "Professionalization and the Social Goals of Architects: A History of the Federation of Architects, Engineers, Chemists and Technicians." In *The Design Professions and the Built Environment*, edited by Paul Knox. New York, NY: Wiley, 2000.

Schön, Donald A. *The Reflective Practitioner: How Professionals Think in Action*. New York, NY: Basic Books, 1983.

—— *Educating the Reflective Practitioner: Toward a New Design for Teaching and Learning in the Professions*. San Francisco: Jossey-Bass, 1990.

Sheldon, Dennis. "Digital Surface Representation and the Constructibility of Gehry's Architecture." PhD Dissertation, Massachusetts Institute of Technology, 2002. Available at http://dspace.mit.edu/handle/1721.1/16899.

Shepard, Mark. *Sentient City: Ubiquitous Computing, Architecture, and the Future of Urban Space*. Cambridge, MA: The MIT Press, 2011.

Sheridan, Thomas B. *Humans and Automation: System Design and Research Issues*. Santa Monica, CA: John Wiley, 2002.

Simon, Herbert Alexander. *The Sciences of the Artificial*. Cambridge, MA: The MIT Press, 1996.

"Simulation." *Oxford Dictionary of English*. Oxford, UK: Oxford University Press, 2010.

Sismondo, Sergio. "Models, Simulations, and Their Objects." *Science in Context* 12(2) (1999): 247–260.

Slaton, Amy E. *Reinforced Concrete and the Modernization of American Building, 1900–1930*. Baltimore: Johns Hopkins University Press, 2001.

Star, Susan Leigh, and Griesemer, James R. "Institutional Ecology, 'Translations' and Boundary Objects: Amateurs and Professionals in Berkeley's Museum of Vertebrate Zoology, 1907–39." *Social Studies of Science* 19(3) (1989): 387–420.

Stiny, George. *Shape: Talking about Seeing and Doing*. Cambridge, MA: The MIT Press, 2008.

Sullivan, Louis H. "The Tall Office Building Artistically Considered." *Lippincott's Magazine* (March 1896).

"Symposium on the Use of Computers." *Arup Newsletter* 17 (November 1963).

Taffs, David. "Computers and the Opera House: Pioneering a New Technology." In *Building a Masterpiece: The Sydney Opera House*, edited by Anne Watson. Sydney: Powerhouse Publishing, 2006: 84–103.

Thompson, Emily. *The Soundscape of Modernity: Architectural Acoustics and the Culture of Listening in America, 1900–1933*. Cambridge, MA: The MIT Press, 2004.

Thomson, Garry. *The Museum Environment*. Oxford, UK: Butterworth-Heinemann, 1978.

Turing, A. M. "On Computable Numbers, with an Application to the Entscheidungsproblem." *Proceedings of the London Mathematical Society* s2–42(1) (January 1937): 230–265.

—— "Computing Machinery and Intelligence." *Mind* LIX(236) (1950): 433–460.

Turkle, Sherry. *Life on the Screen: Identity in the Age of the Internet*. New York, NY: Simon & Schuster, 1995.

—— *The Second Self: Computers and the Human Spirit*. 20th anniversary ed. Cambridge, MA: The MIT Press, 2005.

—— "Always-on/Always-on-you: The Tethered Self." In *Handbook of Mobile Communication Studies*, edited by James E. Katz. Cambridge, MA: The MIT Press, 2008.

—— *The Inner History of Devices*. Cambridge, MA: The MIT Press, 2008.

—— (Ed.) *Simulation and Its Discontents*. Cambridge, MA: The MIT Press, 2009.

—— *Alone Together: Why We Expect More from Technology and Less from Each Other*. 1st ed. New York, NY: Basic Books, 2011.

Turkle, Sherry, and Papert, Seymour. "Epistemological Pluralism and the Revaluation of the Concrete." *Journal of Mathematical Behavior* 11(1) (1992): 3–33.

Turkle, Sherry, and Schön, Donald. *Project Athena at MIT: An Overview*. Cambridge: Massachusetts Institute of Technology, 1988.

Turkle, Sherry, Gusterson, Hugh, Dumit, Joseph, Mindell, David, and Silbey, Susan. *Information Technologies and Professional Identity: A Comparative Study of the Effects of Virtuality*. Report to the National Science Foundation. Cambridge: Massachusetts Institute of Technology, 2005.

Vitruvius. *De Architectura* [Ten Books on Architecture]. Edited by Ingrid D. Rowland and Thomas Noble Howe. Cambridge, UK and New York, NY: Cambridge University Press, 1999.

Wajcman, Judy. "Reflections on Gender and Technology Studies." *Social Studies of Science* 30(3) (June 1, 2000): 447–464.

Weber, Max. *From Max Weber: Essays in Sociology*. Oxford, UK: Oxford University Press, 1946.

Wermiel, Sara E. *The Fireproof Building: Technology and Public Safety in the Nineteenth-Century American City*. Baltimore: The Johns Hopkins University Press, 2000.

Wigley, Mark. "Lost in Space." In *The Critical Landscape*, edited by Michael Speaks. Rotterdam: 010 Publishers, 1996: 30–57.

Williams, A., and Dourish, Paul. "Reimagining the City: The Cultural Dimensions of Urban Computing." *IEEE COMPUTER* 39 (9) 2006: 38–43.

Winsberg, Eric. "Models of Success vs. Success of Models: Reliability without Truth." *Synthese* 152 (2006): 1–19.

—— *Science in the Age of Computer Simulation*. Chicago, IL: University of Chicago Press, 2010.

Wittgenstein, Ludwig. *The Blue and Brown Books*. New York, NY: HarperCollins, 1958.

Woods, Mary N. *From Craft to Profession: The Practice of Architecture in Nineteenth-Century America*. Berkeley: University of California Press, 1999.

Wright, Frank Lloyd. *Frank Lloyd Wright Collected Writings*. New York, NY: Rizzoli, 1992.

Yaneva, Albena. *The Making of a Building: A Pragmatist Approach to Architecture*. Bern: Peter Lang, 2009.

Zalewski, Waclaw, and Allen, Edward. *Shaping Structures: Statics*. Hoboken, NJ: Wiley, 1998.

Index

Page numbers in *italics* denote an illustration